Lessing's *Aesthetica in Nuce*

UNC | COLLEGE OF ARTS AND SCIENCES
Germanic and Slavic Languages and Literatures

From 1949 to 2004, UNC Press and the UNC Department of Germanic & Slavic Languages and Literatures published the UNC Studies in the Germanic Languages and Literatures series. Monographs, anthologies, and critical editions in the series covered an array of topics including medieval and modern literature, theater, linguistics, philology, onomastics, and the history of ideas. Through the generous support of the National Endowment for the Humanities and the Andrew W. Mellon Foundation, books in the series have been reissued in new paperback and open access digital editions. For a complete list of books visit www.uncpress.org.

Lessing's *Aesthetica in Nuce*
An Analysis of the May 26, 1769, Letter to Nicolai

VICTOR ANTHONY RUDOWSKI

UNC Studies in the Germanic Languages and Literatures
Number 69

Copyright © 1971

This work is licensed under a Creative Commons CC BY-NC-ND license. To view a copy of the license, visit http://creativecommons.org/licenses.

Suggested citation: Rudowski, Victor Anthony. *Lessing's Aesthetica in Nuce: An Analysis of the May 26, 1769, Letter to Nicolai.* Chapel Hill: University of North Carolina Press, 1971. DOI: https://doi.org/10.5149/9781469658278_Rudowski

Library of Congress Cataloging-in-Publication Data
Names: Rudowski, Victor Anthony.
Title: Lessing's aesthetica in nuce : An analysis of the May 26, 1769, letter to Nicolai / by Victor Anthony Rudowski.
Other titles: University of North Carolina Studies in the Germanic Languages and Literatures ; no. 69.
Description: Chapel Hill : University of North Carolina Press, [1971] Series: University of North Carolina Studies in the Germanic Languages and Literatures. | Includes bibliographical references.
Identifiers: LCCN 73028576 | ISBN 978-1-4696-5826-1 (pbk: alk. paper) | ISBN 978-1-4696-5827-8 (ebook)
Subjects: Lessing, Gotthold Ephraim, 1729-1781 — Aesthetics. | Aesthetics, German — 18th century.
Classification: LCC PT2415 .R8 | DCC 801/ .93

FOR MY MOTHER AND FATHER

ACKNOWLEDGMENT

The author wishes to express his gratitude to the Harvard University Press for their permission to cite a number of substantive passages from Gerald F. Else's *Aristotle's Poetics: The Argument* both as part of the text itself and in Appendix B.

CONTENTS

I. LESSING'S ARGUMENT TO NICOLAI 1
II. THE AESTHETIC THEORIES OF THE ABBÉ DUBOS 10
III. LESSING'S CONCEPT OF POETRY 20
IV. ARISTOTLE AND THE NECESSITY FOR THEATRICAL PERFORMANCE 34
V. THE NATURE OF ILLUSION 51
VI. THE SUPERIORITY OF THE DRAMA 64
VII. POETRY AS A MIMETIC ART 79
APPENDICES 91
    APPENDIX A: LESSING'S LETTER TO NICOLAI DATED MAY 26, 1769 93
    APPENDIX B: ARISTOTLE'S ARGUMENTS ON THE SUPERIORITY OF THE DRAMA 97
    APPENDIX C: MENDELSSOHN'S "VON DER ILLUSION" 100
NOTES 103
BIBLIOGRAPHY 131

I. LESSING'S ARGUMENT TO NICOLAI

In his letter to Friedrich Nicolai dated April 13, 1769, Lessing expresses profound disappointment over the lack of understanding manifested toward his aesthetic treatise *Laokoon* on the part of contemporary critics. "Da so viele Narren itzt über den Laokoon herfallen," he writes to his friend, "so bin ich nicht übel Willens mich einen Monat oder länger, in Kassel oder Göttingen auf meiner Reise zu verweilen, um ihn zu vollenden. Noch hat sich keiner, auch nicht einmal Herder, träumen lassen, wo ich hinaus will." With respect to Herder's pretense not to have been the author of the extensive critique of *Laokoon* just published in the *Kritische Wälder*, Lessing goes on to assert: "Der Verfasser sey indeß, wer er solle: so ist er doch der einzige, um den es mir der Mühe lohnt, mit meinem Krame ganz an den Tag zu kommen. Es ist mein völliger Ernst, den dritten Theil noch hier [in Hamburg] drucken zu lassen."[1] Despite his resolve to finish work on the proposed trilogy in the immediate future, Lessing never managed to add any further material to the previous notes for the second and third parts that were composed a few months after the publication of Part One in the spring of 1766. These earlier drafts, unfortunately, disclose but little concerning the aesthetic principles alluded to in the remarks to Nicolai cited above. However, in a subsequent letter to Nicolai dated May 26, 1769, Lessing conveniently enters into a detailed discussion of the ideas which he hoped to develop fully within the remaining parts of *Laokoon*. If it is permissible to appropriate the title of Hamann's celebrated treatise for descriptive purposes, the succinct and cohesive argument presented to Nicolai on this occasion may fittingly be characterized as an *aesthetica in nuce*. Although literary scholars have had access to the letter ever since it appeared in the edition of Lessing's collected works published by Nicolai in 1794, it remains imperfectly understood to this day for want of any adequate critical analysis of its contents.[2]

Prior to an examination of the letter itself, however, it is essential to clarify the difference between "natural" and "arbitrary" signs inasmuch as these terms figure prominently in Lessing's argument to Nicolai. Originally set forth in 1719 by the Abbé Dubos in a work entitled *Réflexions critique sur la poésie et sur la peinture*, the distinction between natural and arbitrary signs provides the author of *Laokoon* with one of the key premises in his aesthetic philosophy.[3] Since Dubos fails to discuss either of these concepts in a manner which would permit the citation of formal definitions directly from the *Réflexions*, it is expedient to turn to the writings of Moses Mendelssohn for the sake of a concise explanation. In the treatise *Ueber die Hauptgrundsätze der schönen Künste und Wissenschaften*, which was published in 1761, Mendelssohn argues as follows: "Die Zeichen, vermittelst welcher ein Gegenstand ausgedrückt wird, können entweder natürlich oder willkürlich sein. Natürlich sind sie, wenn die Verbindung des Zeichens mit der bezeichneten Sache in den

Eigenschaften des Bezeichneten selbst gegründet ist... Hingegen werden diejenigen Zeichen willkürlich genannt, die vermöge ihrer Natur mit der bezeichneten Sache nichts gemein haben, aber doch willkürlich dafür angenommen worden sind. Von dieser Art sind die artikulirten Töne aller Sprachen, die Buchstaben, die hieroglyphischen Zeichen der Alten und einige allegorische Bilder, die man mit Recht zu den Hieroglyphen zählen kann."[4] Despite the fact that Mendelssohn is speaking solely on his own behalf, his account of the theory of signs constitutes a reliable summary of the manner in which Dubos' doctrine was interpreted by Lessing and his contemporaries.[5]

Although the terms "natural" and "arbitrary" are employed repeatedly throughout the preliminary drafts for *Laokoon*, they are not overtly mentioned in the final version of Part One. At the opening of the sixteenth chapter, however, Lessing makes implicit use of these concepts in order to draw a fundamental distinction between the aesthetic medium of painting and that of poetry. Here the signs used by the painter are described as "form and color in space" (*Figuren und Farben in dem Raume*), while those at the disposal of the poet are defined as "articulated sounds in time" (*artikulirte Töne in der Zeit*). Obviously, "form and color in space" constitute natural signs, and "articulated sounds in time" (i.e., words) qualify as arbitrary signs. Nevertheless, the argument which Lessing subsequently develops from these postulates does not in any way depend on the natural or arbitrary properties of the signs, but is based entirely on whether the aesthetic medium under consideration is spatial or temporal in character. Because of his adherence to the principle that there must be an appropriate relationship between the signs themselves and the things which they signify, Lessing concludes that the subject matter best suited to painting consists of bodies with their *spatially* coexisting visual attributes. The proper sphere of poetry, in contrast, lies in the realm of *temporally* progressive action (IX, 94-95).

Because the problem of natural and arbitrary signs has little bearing on the issues analyzed in Part One of *Laokoon*, Lessing quite properly felt justified in deferring a full exposition of this aspect of his aesthetic philosophy to another occasion. As a result of its limited scope, the account of the theory of signs to be found in chapter sixteen is readily susceptible to a number of misunderstandings. To begin with, it might appear as though Lessing restricts the painter to working exclusively with natural signs and the poet to operating solely with arbitrary signs. However, in the letter of May 26, 1769 (XVII, 289-292), he openly rejects any rigid dichotomy of this sort. His remarks in this instance pertain to the review of *Laokoon* that was written by Christian Garve for the *Bibliothek der schönen Wissenschaften und der freien Künste* (a journal conducted by Nicolai and Mendelssohn).[6] After informing Nicolai of his general satisfaction with the review, Lessing takes exception to Garve's interpretation of his position on the function of natural as opposed to arbitrary signs and goes on to observe:

> Wenn er [Garve] die Fortsetzung meines Buches wird gelesen haben, soll er wohl finden, daß mich seine Einwürfe nicht treffen. Ich räume ihm ein, daß Verschiedenes darin nicht bestimmt genug ist; aber wie kann es, da ich nur kaum den Einen Unterschied zwischen der Poesie und Malerey zu betrachten angefangen habe, welcher aus dem Gebrauche ihrer Zeichen entspringt, in so fern die einen in der Zeit, und die andern im Raume existiren? Beyde können eben sowohl natürlich, als willkührlich seyn; folglich muß es nothwendig eine doppelte Malerey und eine doppelte Poesie geben: wenigstens von den beyden eine höhere und eine niedrige Gattung.

Quite clearly, the published part of *Laokoon* does little to prepare the reader for the full scope of the aesthetic philosophy of its author.

Since Lessing intends to differentiate between a higher and a lower aesthetic genre on the basis of the theory of signs, he continues his letter by examining the natural and arbitrary qualities of painting and poetry in somewhat more detail than was done in chapter sixteen. Underscoring the complexity of his position, Lessing argues:

> Die Malerey braucht entweder coexistirende

Zeichen, welche natürlich sind, oder welche willkührlich sind; und eben diese Verschiedenheit findet sich auch bey den consecutiven Zeichen der Poesie. Denn es ist eben so wenig wahr, daß die Malerey sich nur natürlicher Zeichen bediene, als es wahr ist, daß die Poesie nur willkührliche Zeichen brauche. Aber das ist gewiß, daß je mehr sich die Malerey von den natürlichen Zeichen entfernt, oder die natürlichen mit willkührlichen vermischt, desto mehr entfernt sie sich von ihrer Vollkommenheit: wie hingegen die Poesie sich um so mehr ihrer Vollkommenheit nähert, je mehr sie ihre willkührlichen Zeichen den natürlichen näher bringt. Folglich ist die höhere Malerey die, welche nichts als natürliche Zeichen im Raume brauchet, und die höhere Poesie die, welche nichts als natürliche Zeichen in der Zeit brauchet. Folglich kann auch weder die historische noch die allegorische Malerey zur höhern Malerey gehören, als welche nur durch die dazu kommenden willkührlichen Zeichen verständlich werden können. Ich nenne aber willkührliche Zeichen in der Malerey nicht allein alles, was zum Costume gehört, sondern auch einen großen Theil des körperlichen Ausdrucks selbst. Zwar sind diese Dinge eigentlich nicht in der Malerey willkührlich; ihre Zeichen sind in der Malerey auch natürliche Zeichen: aber es sind doch *natürliche* Zeichen von *willkührlichen* Dingen, welche unmöglich eben das allgemeine Verständniß, eben die geschwinde und schnelle

Wirkung haben können, als *natürliche* Zeichen von *natürlichen* Dingen.

With respect to Part One of *Laokoon*, Lessing goes on to point out that its argument on painting is restricted solely to the higher form of art, where natural signs are employed to represent natural objects. Since both allegorical and historical painting make use of natural signs to depict arbitrary objects, they belong to the lower category. Accordingly, any discussion of them would have been out of place in Part One. However, Lessing hastens to add that his failure to examine the nature of these lower genres there should not be construed as a total denial of their effectiveness.

Returning to the realm of poetry, Lessing plunges abruptly into an analysis of the process by which words may be elevated to something approaching the status of natural signs. With a degree of urgency, he asserts:

> Nun noch ein Wort von der Poesie, damit Sie nicht mißverstehen, was ich eben gesagt habe. Die Poesie muß schlechterdings ihre willkührlichen Zeichen zu natürlichen zu erheben suchen; und nur dadurch unterscheidet sie sich von der Prose, und wird Poesie. Die Mittel, wodurch sie dieses thut, sind der Ton, die Worte,* die

* In the notes to Volume One of his *History of Modern Criticism*, René Wellek convincingly argues: "The inclusion of 'words' in this list is puzzling. Possibly the letter was not transcribed accurately and should run here,

Stellung der Worte, das Sylbenmaß, Figuren und Tropen, Gleichnisse u.s.w. Alle diese Dinge bringen die willkührlichen Zeichen den natürlichen näher; aber sie machen sie nicht zu natürlichen Zeichen: folglich sind alle Gattungen, die sich nur dieser Mittel bedienen, als die niedern Gattungen der Poesie zu betrachten; und die höchste Gattung der Poesie ist die, welche die willkührlichen Zeichen gänzlich zu natürlichen Zeichen macht. Das ist aber die dramatische; denn in dieser hören die Worte auf willkührliche Zeichen zu seyn, und werden *natürliche* Zeichen willkührlicher Dinge. Daß die dramatische Poesie die höchste, ja die einzige Poesie ist, hat schon Aristoteles gesagt, und er giebt der Epopee nur in so fern die zweyte Stelle, als sie größten Theils dramatisch ist, oder seyn kann. Der Grund, den er davon angiebt, ist zwar nicht der meinige; aber er läßt sich auf meinen reduciren, und wird nur durch diese Reduction auf meinen, vor aller falschen Anwendung gesichert.

Although the system of natural and arbitrary signs still forms the basis of his argument here, Lessing appears to be fully convinced that he is on the threshold of making an important theoretical advance over any previous formulation of this aesthetic doctrine.

'der Ton der Worte'" (p. 304). Henceforth, all references to this section of the letter on my part will presume the validity of the textual emendation suggested by Wellek.

In bringing his letter to a close, Lessing requests Nicolai to solicit Mendelssohn's assessment of these proposals in the following words: "Wenn Sie mit Hrn. Moses eine halbe Stunde darüber plaudern wollen, so melden sie mir doch, was er dazu sagt. Die weitere Ausführung davon soll den dritten Theil meines Laokoons ausmachen."[7] There is no evidence at our disposal, however, which attests to either Mendelssohn's or Nicolai's reactions to the aesthetic philosophy outlined above. Since Lessing never resumes his discussion of these ideas in written form, anyone seeking to resolve the complexities manifested by this letter to Nicolai will find no other primary source materials which are directly related to its argument. Despite these obstacles, several compelling reasons warrant our making a sustained effort to clarify the manner in which Lessing uses the theory of signs on this occasion. First of all, the letter contains his most explicit statement concerning the distinction between poetry and prose. Second, it is the only time that he proposes a way of emending the arguments offered by Aristotle with respect to the superiority of the dramatic over the epic genre. Consequently, a full understanding of these basic issues will not only help to elucidate many aspects of *Laokoon* itself, but will also do much to promote a deeper appreciation of Lessing's literary criticism as a whole.

II. THE AESTHETIC THEORIES OF THE ABBÉ DUBOS

As a first step toward achieving a valid assessment of the merits of Lessing's letter to Nicolai, it will prove advantageous to examine the function of the theory of signs within the context of Dubos' treatise on poetry and painting. Since the most frequently cited part of the *Réflexions* involves the instance in which aesthetic experience is equated to a gustatory one, an analysis of the treatise may properly open with a consideration of this celebrated passage. Here Dubos begins by asking rhetorically:

> Raisonne-t'on ... pour décider si le ragoût est bon? On n'en fait rien. Il est en nous un sens fait pour connoître si le Cusinier a operé suivant les regles de son art. On goûte le ragoût, & même sans sçavoir ces regles, on connoît s'il est bon. Il en est de même en quelque maniere des ouvrages d'esprit & des tableaux faits pour nous plaire en nous touchant ... Lorsqu'il s'agit de connoître si l'imitation qu'on nous présente dans un poëme ou dans la composition d'un tableau, est capable d'exciter la compassion & d'attendrir, le sens destiné pour en juger, est le sens même qui auroit été attendri, c'est le sens qui auroit jugé de l'objet imité. C'est ce sixiéme sens qui est en nous, sans que nous voïions ses organes. C'est la portion de nous-mêmes qui juge sur l'impression qu'elle ressent, & qui, pour me servir des termes de Platon,* prononce, sans consulter le regle

---

* In a note to this passage, Dubos refers the reader to Bk. X of Plato's *Republic*.

& le compas. C'est enfin ce qu'on appelle communément le sentiment.[1]

Although Dubos mitigates his otherwise extreme sensationalism by appealing to the vague existence of a sixth sense, it should be noted that this sense too operates on the same non-intellectual basis as do the other sense organs with which man is endowed.

Underlying this view of aesthetic enjoyment is the classification of mental activity which is described in the first chapter of the *Réflexions*. Here Dubos divides the operations of the mind into the meditative (or reflective) and sensual categories. According to Dubos' theory, mental activity of the meditative variety requires an exertion of the will, and it is therefore inevitable that man finds himself unable to sustain this type of intellectual tension for long without experiencing mental fatigue. Hence, he is obliged to keep his meditative powers in a state of suspension most of the time. Rather than succumb to the oppressive boredom which results from an inactive mind, man seeks occasion for the engagement of his mental faculties by consciously surrendering himself to external experiences that are capable of arousing his emotions. In section two of Part One, Dubos attributes the pleasure which mankind derives from witnessing gruesome spectacles like gladiatorial matches, bullfights, or public executions to the fact that the misfortunes of fellow creatures naturally arouse our passions and that any exercise of our emotions is pleasurable in and of itself.

Since Dubos freely concedes that the artistic imitation of objects and events can never hope to arouse an emotional response that is equal in intensity to the one induced by their prototypes in life, he must explain why man is willing to accept the weaker emotions engendered by art as a substitute for the greater vividness of experiences provided by the real world. Dubos therefore devotes the third section of Part One of the *Réflexions* to demonstrating that man not only accepts the simulated passions produced by art as a substitute for their counterpart in reality, but actually prefers the former to the latter. By way of justifying this preference, Dubos maintains that the pleasure of indulging our passions in real life is followed by a period of unhappiness that is of longer duration. Because art stimulates emotions similar in quality to natural sensation, but which are felt to be artificial on account of their inferior force, art enables man to engage the non-reflective aspect of his mind and at the same time to divorce himself from the unhappy consequences which normally follow similar experiences in real life. The fact that man is always conscious that art is imitation, never reality, also permits him to enjoy the depiction of things and occurrences which would be succeeded by extreme emotional discomfiture had they really existed or really taken place.

In section ten of Part One Dubos maintains

that the enjoyment obtained from an imitation must always be of a lower emotional intensity than the pleasure resulting from an actual encounter with the same objects or events. Since the intensity of feeling produced by an aesthetic imitation is directly proportional to that aroused by its counterpart in real life, it follows that a poet or painter should attempt to imitate subjects which are emotionally engaging in reality. Because tragic situations in life excite a more intense emotional response than do comic ones, more enjoyment is derived from tragedies than from comedies and herein lies the superiority of the former genre over the latter. Dubos insists, furthermore, than nothing which does not arouse our passions in reality can affect us in an imitation. In adherence to the type of aesthetic humanism espoused by his compatriot André Félibien,[2] Dubos also expresses disapproval of still-life and landscape painting, but nevertheless concedes that these forms of art often inspire our admiration. By carefully distinguishing between the pleasure occasioned by our admiration for the imitative skill of the artist and the pleasure arising from the aesthetic experience itself, Dubos is able to explain away this apparent contradiction of his previous thesis. Although it may superficially appear as though such uninteresting scenes as those depicted by the still-life and landscape painter actually engage the viewer sensually, the true explanation is that the imitative skill displayed in the execution of these pictures evokes feelings of admiration for the artist himself, and these feelings in no way constitute evidence of an interest in the subject matter as such.

This distinction emphasizes the fact that the sense experience induced by a work of art is fully independent and autonomous and, like any other form of sense experience, carries no reference to anything outside itself. While it utilizes the elements of ordinary experience as building blocks, art establishes its own universe of discourse which is entirely separate from the world around us. Although Dubos considers all art to be an imitation of nature, he refuses to concede that aesthetic enjoyment requires either an explicit or implicit act of comparison from a work of art to its counterpart in reality. According to Dubos, such a postulate is ruled out *a priori* since all aesthetic experience is the product of the sensual side of man's nature. Whenever a work of art evokes an act of comparison on the part of the observer – as is the case where a landscape or still-life painter arouses our admiration for his imitative skill, it is the meditative or reflective variety of mental activity that is being employed and not the sensual. In contemplating a completely successful imitation of nature, however, one is usually conscious of neither the imitator nor the object of imitation, but solely of the imitation itself.

Since the sensations experienced through the medium of art never attain the degree of intensity which characterizes the sensual experiences of real life, there is scarcely any danger of confusing one type of sensation with the other. Dubos holds that the distinction between imitation and reality is manifest in all forms of the plastic arts and in all literary genres, including the dramatic. Even the performance of a play with living actors and realistic scenery can never convince a spectator who is in full possession of his faculties that the event taking place on the stage is a real occurrence and make him forget that he is only watching an imitation of an action. In the forty-third section of the first part of the *Réflexions*, which is entitled "Que le plaisir que nous avons au Théatre, n'est point produit par l'illusion," Dubos emphatically denies that "l'appareil de la Scene & la déclamation des Acteurs nous imposent assez pour nous faire croire, qu'au lieu d'assister à la représentation de l'évenement, nous assistons à l'évenement même, & que nous voïons réellement l'action, & non pas une imitation" (I, 421-422).

Despite his conviction that complete illusion can never be attained by means of the imitative processes of art, Dubos maintains that the excellence of a work of art is directly proportional to the forcefulness of the impression it creates. In the fortieth section of Part One of the *Réflexions* he attempts to establish the superiority of painting over poetry on this basis and advances two reasons for his belief that painting produces effects greater than those of poetry. The first reason is that it operates on us by means of the sense of sight. "La vûë a plus d'empire sur l'ame," he declares, "que les autre sens ... On peut dire, métaphoriquement parlant, que l'œil est plus près de l'ame que l'oreille" (I, 387). Although closely related to the above argument, Dubos' second reason is based on the theory of signs. Because he holds that natural signs are intrinsically more forceful than arbitrary ones, Dubos seeks to demonstrate the superiority of painting by arguing: "La Peinture emploïe des signes naturels dont l'énergie ne dépend pas de l'éducation. Ils tirent leur force du rapport que la nature elle-même a pris soin de mettre entre les objets extérieurs & nos organes, afin de procurer notre conservation. Je parle peut-être mal, quand je dis que la Peinture emploïe des signes. C'est la nature elle-même que la Peinture met sous nos yeux ... La figure des objets, leur couleur, les reflais de la lumiere, les ombres, enfin tout ce que l'œil peut appercevoir, se trouve dans un tableau comme nous le voïons dans la nature. Elle se présente dans un tableau sous la même forme où nous la voïons réellement" (I, 388). Since language is a system of arbitrary signs, Dubos contends that poetry is unable to operate with the directness of nature. In Dubos' judgment, the process of converting the potential energy in words into the kinetic energy of sensation is characterized by a high coefficient of friction, and verbal description is for this reason inherently inefficient. A scene represented in painting must, all other factors being equal, produce a more

vivid response than its counterpart in poetry.
    While Dubos concedes that dramas depicting tragic events are capable of arousing passions more intense than those stimulated by painting, he does not consider his belief in the superiority of painting over poetry to be contradicted by this fact. Here again he has a twofold answer. First, he maintains that the forceful impression resulting from a stage performance of a tragedy is produced by means of the eye and points out that the effect of tragedy is greatly diminished if it is merely read in private. Second, since a tragedy on the stage actually becomes an infinite series of pictures, it is easy to understand how the cumulative effect of the series makes a more forceful impression than an individual painting, which is, of necessity, confined to the representation of but a single instant in time. For these two reasons, Dubos concludes that tragedy owes its greater vividness to the natural signs perceived during a performance and not to the arbitrary signs of the dialogue.
    Although Dubos and Lessing are in complete agreement regarding the pre-eminence of drama among the literary genres, their reasons for holding this view are totally dissimilar. Being a creative writer as well as a literary critic, Lessing could hardly be expected to accept Dubos' contention that poetry is innately inferior to the plastic arts as a medium of aesthetic communication. Admittedly, it is difficult to see how Lessing can avoid coming to a similar conclusion since he

himself fully agrees with Dubos' argument concerning the greater efficacy of natural as opposed to arbitrary signs. In the earliest draft of *Laokoon*, for example, Lessing declares: "Da Figuren und Farben natürliche Zeichen sind, die Worte hingegen, durch welche wir Figuren und Farben ausdrücken nicht, so müßen die Wirkungen der Kunst, welche jene braucht unendlich geschwinder und lebhafter seyn, als die einer, die sich mit diesen begnügen muß" (XIV, 336). But in the next paragraph, he goes on to compensate the poet for the inferior ability of arbitrary signs to evoke form and color by pointing out: "Bewegungen können durch Worte lebhafter ausgedrückt werden, als Farben und Figuren; folglich wird der Dichter seine körperlichen Gegenstände mehr durch jene als durch diese sinnlich zu machen suchen" (XIV, 336). By virtue of the temporal nature of his medium, the poet is thus able to imitate a variety of progressive actions that lie beyond the scope of the plastic arts. Underscoring the manner in which this limitation of painting and sculpture affects their status as imitative arts, Harlan P. Hanson asserts: "Basic to the argument of *Laokoon* is the silent premise that the timeless nature of the plastic arts ... relegates therewith the entire domain to an inferior status."[3] Despite the cogency of the solution suggested by this latent premise, it in no way represents Lessing's total response to the arguments by which Dubos sought to demonstrate the superiority of painting. As Lessing was later to explain to Nicolai, the poet has devices at his disposal which enable him to transform the arbitrary signs of ordinary language to the natural signs associated with sensate experience. Moreover, Lessing insists that unless words are made to function in the manner of natural signs, the poet cannot properly be said to have elevated language from the status of prose to that of poetry.

III. LESSING'S CONCEPT OF POETRY

Perhaps the easiest way to clarify the manner in which Lessing differentiates poetry from prose is to reformulate his argument in terms of a contemporary aesthetic system which employs concepts that are analogous to the distinction between natural and arbitrary signs. By characterizing the poetic process as an endeavor to convert arbitrary into natural signs, Lessing is, in effect, expressing a view of the nature of poetry which is remarkably similar to the one recently advanced by Susanne K. Langer in *Philosophy in a New Key*. In this work, which was first published in 1942, Mrs. Langer distinguishes between poetry and prose on the basis of the proposition that poetic discourse aims to transmit "presentational" knowledge, while prose discourse seeks to convey "discursive" knowledge. As she explains these terms, discursive knowledge derives its meaning from the fixed denotation of words and from the syntactical and logical structure of language; it is, consequently, general and abstract. Presentational knowledge, on the other hand, is particular and concrete in the fashion of the aesthetic experience communicated by painting and sculpture. Although the poet employs a discursive medium, Mrs. Langer insists that he too is able to impart presentational knowledge. "The material of poetry is discursive," she argues, "but the product – artistic phenomenon – is not..."[1] In terms of her analysis, it is not the literal (discursive) assertion which is made in words that invests a poem with artistic meaning, but rather the imagery and other forms of presentational symbolism which a poetic manipulation of language can invoke (pp. 260-261). The prime task of a poet, accordingly, is to use speech in such a way as to cause the conventional aspects of language to be displaced by aesthetic qualities of the non-verbal type, one form of which is to be found in the visual arts.[2]

Several passages in *Laokoon* attest to a similar conviction on Lessing's part. In the seventeenth chapter, for example, Lessing delineates the qualities for which the poet must strive if he is to transcend the limitations of prose discourse as follows: "Der Poet will nicht bloß verständlich werden, seine Vorstellungen sollen nicht bloß klar und deutlich seyn; hiermit begnügt sich der Prosaist. Sondern er will die Ideen, die er in uns erwecket, so lebhaft machen, daß wir in der Geschwindigkeit die wahren sinnlichen Eindrücke ihrer Gegenstände zu empfinden glauben, und in diesem Augenblicke der Täuschung, uns der Mittel, die er dazu anwendet, seiner Worte bewußt zu seyn aufhören" (IX, 101). With this objective in mind, Lessing goes on to recommend that "der Dichter soll immer mahlen" and refers the reader to the definition of poetic painting which was previously given in the fourteenth chapter of *Laokoon*. There he asserts that "jeder Zug, jede Verbindung mehrerer Züge, durch die uns der Dichter seinen Gegenstand so sinnlich macht, daß wir uns dieses Gegenstandes deutlicher bewußt werden, als seiner Worte, heißt mahlerisch, heißt ein Gemählde, weil es uns dem Grade der Illusion näher bringt, dessen das materielle Gemählde besonders fähig ist, der sich von dem materiellen Gemählde am ersten und leichtesten abstrahiren lassen" (IX, 92). If the process described in these passages were to be reformulated in terms of Mrs. Langer's aesthetic philosophy, the function of a poet might be said to consist in transforming discursive symbolism into presentational symbolism. This is also what Lessing means when he maintains that poetry must try to raise its arbitrary signs to natural signs.

Among the devices which are at a poet's disposal for the purpose of rendering a reader more aware of the sensual properties of poetry and less conscious of its verbal medium, Lessing specifically refers Nicolai to such items as the tone of words, the position of words, measure, figures and tropes, and similes. Although these techniques are also discussed within *Philosophy in a New Key*, Mrs. Langer's remarks concerning their aesthetic significance do not lend themselves to direct citation. However, in the book entitled *Homer and the Heroic Tradition* (Cambridge, Mass., 1958), Cedric Whitman provides his readers with a short account of Susanne Langer's views on the poetic function of language which may serve in lieu of her own observations on the topic. By way of summary, Whitman writes:

> Any word alone may be imagistic, except perhaps colorless modal auxiliaries, and any

word may be a poetic symbol, hence presentational. But when a group of grammatically related words become presentational, it is because some technique has been employed to supress their grammatical symbolism... The techniques which tend to identify groups of words with artistic rather than logical syntax are familiar: metaphor and other figures, departure from colloquial order of words, actual omission of some grammatical factor which can be easily understood, meter with its effect of contrapuntally modifying the normal sound of words, rhyme which tends to emphasize sound over sense, and finally diction. (p. 107)

The similarity of Lessing's and Mrs. Langer's formulation of the poetic process is too obvious to require further comment.

In view of her own numerous expressions of indebtedness to the theories of Ernst Cassirer, Alfred Whitehead, Ludwig Wittgenstein, and other leading twentieth-century thinkers, it is also unnecessary to argue the fact that the aesthetic doctrines propounded by Susanne Langer are fully abreast of the most significant developments in contemporary philosophy. Because the theoretical framework of *Laokoon* is analogous to the symbolic system adopted by Mrs. Langer, it might at first appear as though the aesthetic orientation of Lessing was largely independent of the main currents of German philosophic thought in his own era. However, further analysis of

Lessing's ideas will reveal that his theory of art is fully compatible with the major tenets of Christian Wolff's version of Leibnizian philosophy; a system of thought then dominant in mid-eighteenth-century Germany and popularly termed *Weltweisheit*.[3] Among the adherents of Wolffian philosophy, Alexander Gottlieb Baumgarten in particular deserves recognition for having formulated an aesthetic doctrine which has much in common with contemporary trends in literary and artistic criticism. Indeed, the cycle running from the aesthetic views of Baumgarten to those recently espoused by Mrs. Langer represents a return to a cognitive explanation of artistic communication after an intervening period of almost two centuries during which theories of art stressing the expression of emotion have been in dominance.[4]

No true appreciation of the relationship between the ideas of Baumgarten and those of Lessing is possible, however, without at least a rudimentary acquaintance with the epistemological system which the *Weltweisen* derived from the philosophy of Leibniz. In the essay entitled *Meditationes de cognitione, veritate, et ideis* (1684), perhaps the fullest exposition of his theory of knowledge, Leibniz commences by distinguishing between concepts (*notiones*) that are clear (*clarae*) and those which are obscure (*obscurae*). "A concept is obscure," he states, "which does not suffice for recognizing the thing represented, as when I merely remember some flower or animal which I have once seen but not well enough to recognize it when it is placed before me and to distinguish it from similar ones."[5] From this definition it follows that obscure concepts can play no role in the cognitive process and are therefore to be excluded from the sphere of philosophic inquiry. When it is possible to distinguish an idea from others of its kind, Leibniz classifies the mental phenomenon as a clear concept.

Clear concepts are likewise divided into two categories and are characterized by Leibniz as either confused (*confusae*) or distinct (*distinctae*).[6] An example which is often used to illustrate the difference between these two types of clarity involves the formulation of a definition of gold. One way of defining the concept of gold would be to enumerate a sufficient number of its sensual attributes – its color, its hardness, its malleability, etc. Such an approach is the way of confused cognition, because the qualities listed are not internally analyzable. What this means is simply that it is impossible to explain these terms to anyone who has never experienced them. "So we cannot explain to a blind man what red is," Leibniz writes, "nor can we explain such a quality to others except by bringing them into the presence of the thing and making them see, smell or taste it, or at least by reminding them of some similar perception they have had in the past."[7] A concept of gold that is distinct would, on the other hand, be of the kind employed by physicists and chemists. In accordance with these epistemological principles, the operations of the cognitive faculties are divided by most proponents of *Weltweisheit* into two categories: a higher (intellectual) part whose ideas are *clear and distinct* and a lower (perceptual) part whose ideas are *clear and confused*.[8] This division of cognitive mental activity, it must be stressed, is one which corresponds in all essential respects to the distinction between presentational and discursive symbolism that is set forth by Mrs. Langer in *Philosophy in a New Key*.

Baumgarten fully accepts the epistemological framework outlined above and he, like Leibniz and Wolff, holds that poetry and the fine arts are products of the lower (perceptual) faculties of cognition and express concepts which are clear and confused. Although his theories were developed within the context of orthodox *Weltweisheit*, Baumgarten departs from the intellectual perspective of his philosophic mentors by placing a far greater value on artistic cognition. So as to expand the range of philosophic inquiry among the *Weltweisen*, he proposes to establish a science dealing with clear and confused concepts which is to take its place alongside Logic, the science dealing with clear and distinct concepts. Using the Greek verb meaning "to perceive" as a basis, Baumgarten gives the new science of confused perception the name of Aesthetics. This designation was originally employed by Baumgarten near the end of the essay entitled *Meditationes philosophicae de nonnullis ad poema pertinentibus*, a work published in 1735 when its author was only twenty years of age. He later chose the name *Aesthetica* as the title for a proposed trilogy in which the doctrines set forth in the earlier treatise were to be elaborated and extended. The first volume was published in 1750, and the second in 1758. However, owing to the author's death in 1762, the third volume never appeared and the work remains incomplete.

While it is universally acknowledged that Lessing was influenced by Baumgarten, the extent of his indebtedness is more difficult to determine. According to Erich Schmidt, both Lessing and Mendelssohn profited from the study of Baumgarten's writings which they jointly undertook in the seventeen-fifties, although neither of them ever became a completely loyal adherent of his system.[9] Of all Lessing's writings, Schmidt feels that the *Abhandlungen über die Fabel*, which were published in 1758, show the greatest intellectual commitment to the theories of Baumgarten and Wolff (Schmidt, I, 379). He goes on to point out, however, that this dependence gradually diminishes as both Lessing and Mendelssohn become acquainted with the works of Shaftesbury, Burke, and other British aestheticians, after which time they increasingly adopt the empirical approach prevalent on that side of the channel in preference to the deductive methodology of Baumgarten and Dubos (Schmidt, I, 252, 473). Reflecting the spirit of this trend toward induction, the introduction to *Laokoon* contains the following description of the manner in which its author developed the principles set forth in the main body of the text: "Sie sind zufälliger Weise entstanden, und mehr nach der Folge meiner Lectüre, als durch die methodische Entwickelung allgemeiner Grundsätze angewachsen. Es sind also mehr unordentliche Collectanea zu einem Buche, als ein Buch" (IX, 5). And a few sentences further on, there appears the sole reference to Baumgarten which is to be found in *Laokoon*. "Baumgarten bekannte," Lessing informs us, "einen grossen Theil der Beyspiele in seiner Aesthetik, Gesners Wörterbuche* schuldig zu seyn. Wenn mein Raisonnement nicht so bündig ist als das Baumgartensche, so werden doch meine Beyspiele mehr nach der Quelle schmecken" (IX, 5). Although these remarks tend to corroborate Schmidt's assessment of Lessing's methodological development, it should be pointed out that Lessing never entirely abandoned deductive argumentation and that the principles enunciated in chapter sixteen of *Laokoon* are arrived at by means of reasoning from general premises to particular conclusions.

To judge from the terminology employed in *Laokoon* and its extant drafts, moreover, it also appears safe to conclude that the influence of the *Weltweisen* on Lessing never waned to the point where he felt obliged to abandon the epistemological system outlined above. In order to be in a position to recognize Lessing's continuing com-

* By *Gesners Wörterbuch*, Lessing is referring to Johann Mathias Gesner's *Novus linguae et eruditionis Romanae Thesaurus*, which was published at Leipzig in 1747-48.

mitment to this scheme, one aspect of his terminology needs to be clarified. Although he deems it fitting to retain the terms "clear" (*klar*), "distinct" (*deutlich*), and "obscure" (*dunkel*), Lessing chooses to rid himself of the misleading expression "confused" (*verworren*) by substituting a more appropriate equivalent in the form of the word "sensuous" (*sinnlich*). It would be a mistake to give Lessing exclusive credit for having improved the terminology in this respect, however, since ample precedent for the change may be found in the writings of the *Weltweisen* themselves. Baumgarten, perhaps more clearly than others, equates the term "confused" with the word "sensuous" and uses the two expressions interchangeably throughout his writings.[10] Interestingly enough, Baumgarten also prefers to define aesthetics as the "science of *sensuous* (or sensate) cognition" (*scientia cognitionis sensitivae*) and poetry as "perfect *sensuous* (or sensate) discourse" (*oratio sensitiva perfecta*). Unfortunately, he makes no attempt to justify his preference for the word "sensuous" over the term "confused" when these definitions are introduced in the *Meditationes*. Whatever the reasons for Baumgarten's choice, however, both of these definitions have the clear advantage of implying that "confused" concepts in the realm of aesthetics should not only *appeal* to sensuous concepts for their ideational content, but must also *evoke* those self-same sense qualities in the mind of an individual who contemplates a painting or peruses a poem.[11]

Although the terms "clear" and "distinct" are used sparingly in the published part of *Laokoon*, they are always employed in a manner which conforms to the meaning invested in them by the *Weltweisen*.[12] A passage in the earliest draft of *Laokoon*, moreover, substantiates Lessing's continuing adherence to Baumgarten's epistemological principles even more convincingly than any part of the published version. Lessing's remarks on this occasion concern the description of Agamemnon given in one of the early books of the *Iliad* in which Homer is apparently guilty of indulging in the enumeration of coexisting parts. Here Homer writes: "In the center rode Agamemnon: he had a frown worthy of Zeus, a waist worthy of Ares, a breast worthy of Poseidon! He reminded everyone of a bull, standing nobly prepared to defend his herd; so heroic and grand, by the grace of Heaven was his appearance."[13] By way of absolving Homer of the charge that he employed a prose writer's method of description, Lessing argues: "Wenn Homer ja einen schönen oder erhabenen Gegenstand durch die Beschreibung seiner einzeln Theile neben einander schildert, so bedienet er sich dabey eines sehr merkwürdigen Kunstgriffes; nehmlich er füget so fort ein Gleichniß bey, in welchem wir den zergliederten Gegenstand wieder beysammen erblicken, welcher den erlangten deutlichen Begriff wieder verwischt und dem Gegenstande nichts als eine sinnliche Klarheit läßt."[14] Thus by means of the deferred simile, Homer has, in Lessing's eyes, been able to integrate the separate elements employed in his description of Agamemnon into a single poetic image and hence to counteract the distinctness inherent in the technique of enumerating coexistent parts.

In connection with his discussion of Homer's use of the deferred simile, Lessing goes on to censure Alexander Pope's translation of the description of Agamemnon and maintains that the Englishman destroyed its efficacy "indem er diesen Kunstgriff nicht gefühlt, und das Gleichniß vorannimmt" (XIV, 337). Pope's translation runs as follows:

Like some proud bull that round the pasture leads
His subject herds, the monarch of the meads.
Great as the gods, the exalted mien was seen,
His strength like Neptune, and like Mars his mien:
Jove o'er his eyes celestial glories spread,
And dawning conquest play'd around his head.
                    (Bk. II, ll. 566-571)

In rendering this passage into English, Pope has, in Lessing's judgment, significantly reduced the sensual content of Homer's description of Agamemnon as a result of having transposed the unifying simile from a terminal to an initial position within the series. Lessing's criticism of Pope's translation, quite obviously, stems directly from his adherence to Baumgarten's tenet that poetry is sensuous discourse perfected.

In addition to the use of metaphor and other

tropes, Baumgarten emphasizes the function of such devices as meter, rhyme, and diction as a means of transforming language into an instrument of sensuous cognition. One notable deficiency in Baumgarten's philosophy of art, however, is the absence of a semiotic system which is capable of differentiating between the various aesthetic media.[15] It was to compensate for this omission that Lessing turned to the Abbé Dubos' theory of signs. But he could not accept Dubos' theory of signs in its entirety for good reason. While Dubos and Lessing are in full agreement in regard to the sensuous nature of aesthetic imitation, they differ greatly on the relative merits of poetry and the plastic arts as mimetic media. By virtue of the fact that natural signs are intrinsically more forceful than arbitrary ones, Dubos maintains that the plastic arts have an enormous advantage over those employing a purely verbal medium. In order to counteract this argument, Lessing endeavored to reformulate the theory of signs in such a way as to overcome the rigid semiotic dichotomy through which the poet was restricted to the use of arbitrary signs. Unlike other eighteenth-century writers on aesthetics who adopted Dubos' theory of signs, Lessing argued that it was possible for the arbitrary signs of ordinary language to be converted into natural ones by means of the poetic process (or at least to come extremely close to that status). Thus he more than anyone else was able to undermine the effectiveness of the argument that poetry is inferior to the plastic arts on account of the arbitrary nature of its medium.

In short, Lessing's concept of poetry may be viewed as a truly organic synthesis of ideas derived from the works of Dubos and Baumgarten. Although the theories of both men are constructed on the assumption that the function of poetry is to communicate what is now termed "presentational" knowledge, each exhibits a deficiency for which the other offers a means of compensation. From Lessing's point of view, Dubos underestimates the capacity of language to convey sensuous experience through "arbitrary" signs and overvalues the advantages enjoyed by the plastic arts because of their overt use of "natural" signs. Baumgarten, in contrast, fully recognizes the potentialities of poetry as a vehicle for sensuous discourse, but fails to investigate the aesthetic consequences arising from the fact that the verbal and plastic arts employ different media (or signs) for the purpose of sensual communication. By amalgamating the most viable elements in their respective positions, Lessing was able to remedy the shortcomings which they manifest individually and to create a theory of poetry which so easily fits in among the aesthetic philosophies of the twentieth century.[16]

IV. ARISTOTLE AND THE NECESSITY FOR THEATRICAL PERFORMANCE

In the previously-cited letter to Nicolai dated May 26, 1769, Lessing contends that drama is superior to all other forms of literature because only within its context do words truly become "natürliche Zeichen willkührlicher Dinge." As part of the general exposition of Lessing's literary theories in his *History of Modern Criticism*, René Wellek interprets this passage from the letter to mean that language in a play "is natural because it is spoken *by* characters and *in* character, with gestures and expressions of the face as in real life" (I, 165). In a study published a few years later, Elida Maria Szarota, who is fully cognizant of Wellek's position, makes the same point by observing: "Die Schauspielkunst ist ja als solche bereits die Kunst, in der die 'willkürlichen' Zeichen – dank den Gesten und der Mimik der Schauspielkunst – von selbst zu 'natürlichen' Zeichen werden."[1] A similar interpretation may also be found in Emil Gottschlich's *Lessing's aristotelische Studien*, which was published in 1876.[2] In order to assess the validity of this solution properly, it is necessary to recall that Lessing himself stresses the compatibility of his own views regarding the superiority of the drama with those advanced by Aristotle. "Der Grund, den er [Aristotle] davon angiebt, ist zwar nicht der meinige," Lessing concedes, "aber er läßt sich auf meinen reduciren, und wird nur durch diese Reduction auf meinen, vor aller falschen Anwendung gesichert." Hence, while any interpretation of Lessing's proposition may legitimately *differ* from the views propounded by Aristotle, it should not actually *conflict* with them.

Unlike Wellek and Miss Szarota, Gottschlich attempts to relate his interpretation of Lessing's position to the doctrines formulated by Aristotle. Drawing upon the arguments advanced in the *Poetics* with respect to the superiority of tragedy over the epic, Gottschlich holds that Lessing's proposal must have been prompted by the passage where Aristotle asserts: "Then further, because it has everything the epic has (it can even use its verse), and no small element besides: the music and the effects of spectacle, through which the spectator's enjoyment is most vividly aroused."[3] In an attempt to achieve the reduction proposed by Lessing, Gottschlich connects Aristotle's reference to the effects of spectacle (i.e., performance) with the theory of signs by means of the following argument: "Wenn Lessing es für möglich erklärt, den von Aristoteles angegebenen Grund auf den seinigen, nach welchem der dramatischen Kunst insofern der Vorrang vor den übrigen Gattungen der Dichtkunst gebührt, weil dieselbe die Worte zu natürlichen Zeichen der Dinge erhebt, zu reducieren, so kann er, was zunächst den zweiten von Aristoteles angegebenen Gesichtspunkt, nämlich die theatralische Darstellung betrifft, nur die mimischen Bewegungen des Schauspielers, welche die Worte begleiten, als natürliche Zeichen der Empfindung in Betracht gezogen haben" (p. 128). Gottschlich also believes that this interpretation is corroborated by a passage in the fourth article of the *Hamburgische Dramaturgie*. Here Lessing compares the type of gesticulation utilized by the ancients in the pantomime with the kind that they employed in normal acting and observes: "Die Hände des Schauspielers waren bey weitem so geschwätzig nicht, als die Hände des Pantomimens. Bey diesem vertraten sie die Stelle der Sprache; bey jenem sollten sie nur den Nachdruck derselben vermehren und durch ihre Bewegungen, als natürliche Zeichen der Dinge, den verabredeten Zeichen der Stimme Wahrheit und Leben verschaffen helfen" (IX, 197-198). The next sentence in the above passage, although Gottschlich does not refer to it directly, is also relevant to the issue and worthy of citation. "Bey dem Pantomimen," Lessing further stipulates, "waren die Bewegungen der Hände nicht blos natürliche Zeichen; viele derselben hatten eine conventionelle Bedeutung, und dieser mußte sich der Schauspieler gänzlich enthalten" (IX, 198).

As a supplementary argument, Gottschlich goes on to contend that words may also attain the status of natural signs by having their effect reinforced through musical accompaniment – music being a medium of aesthetic communication which, according to both Lessing and Dubos, employs natural signs.[4] In support of this hypothesis, Gottschlich refers to one of the drafts for *Laokoon* in which Lessing expresses a desire to see a restoration of the kind of unity between music and word that once typified Greek drama. In a passage where he deplores the separation of the arts of music and poetry practised by his contemporaries, Lessing actually goes far toward anticipating the aesthetic views of Richard Wagner.[5] "Es hat auch wirklich eine Zeit gegeben," Lessing writes, "wo sie beyde zusammen nur eine Kunst ausmachten. Ich will indeß nicht leugnen, daß die Trennung nicht natürlich erfolgt sey... aber ich darf doch betauern, daß durch diese Trennung man an die Verbindung fast gar nicht mehr denkt, oder wenn man ja noch daran denkt, man die eine Kunst nur zu einer Hilfskunst der andern macht, und von einer gemeinschaftlichen Wirkung, welche beyde zu gleichen Theilen hervorbringen, gar nichts mehr weis" (XIV, 431). Because of its subordination of the libretto to the musical score, Lessing did not regard the opera of his day as having achieved the symbiotic balance between music and the spoken word which was once characteristic of the antique theater (XIV, 432).

Thus in carrying out Lessing's suggestion that Aristotle's arguments on the superiority of the drama be reduced to the theory of signs, Gottschlich takes the position that the arbitrary signs which make up the dialogue of a Greek play attain the status of natural signs when they are used in conjunction with the mimetic gestures of actors and to the accompaniment of music – either reason being sufficient in itself. Since modern European plays are normally performed without musical accompaniment, that part of Gottschlich's exegesis which is derived from the example of music cannot make any contribution toward an elucidation of Lessing's thesis regarding the superiority of the dramatic form and may therefore be left out of consideration. The relevant portion of Gottschlich's interpretation pertains to the mimetic gestures of actors and is essentially the same as the proposal advanced by Wellek. Although Gottschlich endeavors to substantiate this aspect of his interpretation of Lessing's remarks to Nicolai by citing corroborative passages from both the *Poetics* and the *Hamburgische Dramaturgie*, his most cogent argument is derived from the latter work. In view of the fact that Lessing refers to the mimetic gestures of actors as "natürliche Zeichen der Dinge" in the fourth article of the *Dramaturgie*, Gottschlich feels justified in interpreting the expression "natürliche Zeichen willkührlicher Dinge" in a similar fashion.

Since Lessing insists that his explanation in no way conflicts with the theories of Aristotle, Gottschlich's hypothesis needs to be examined in the context of the arguments on the superiority of tragedy set forth in the *Poetics*. In order to comprehend these arguments fully, it is important to bear in mind that they are in part directed against Plato, who regarded the epic as superior to the drama. In the dialogue entitled *Laws*, for example, Plato holds that the drama's appeal is more vulgar than that of the epic. Although both are communicated orally, the one acted and the other recited, the epic manifests its superiority by appealing to the better type of citizen, that is, the old men. The old men are best educated and are better listeners than other age groups. Such an audience, Plato asserts in an apparent reference to the graphic nature of acting and the dance, have no need of gestures.[6] In addition to the objections against the drama specifically raised by Plato, Aristotle also takes note of the commonly-made criticisms that the movements of the actors are often excessive and exaggerated to the point of vulgarity and that characters of a low type are frequently depicted in tragedy (*Poetics*, 1461b).

In order to refute the aforementioned charges, Aristotle makes a systematic comparison between the dramatic and epic genres and establishes seven counter-arguments in favor of the drama. One of these counter-arguments has already been cited in full in connection with Gottschlich's attempt to reduce the reasons set forth in the *Poetics* to the theory of signs.[7] Before any of the remaining counter-arguments are cited directly, however, it will prove advantageous to review all seven briefly by consulting the outline to be found in Gerald F. Else's highly-esteemed commentary entitled *Aristotle's Poetics: The Argument*. Summing up the Stagirite's position, Else writes:

> Aristotle presents seven counter-arguments, some brief and relatively less important, some (especially the next to the last) much more elaborate and decisive:
>
> 1 (a4-7). The charge [that actors indulge in a

plethora of movement] lies against the art of acting, not that of poetry, and can be made with the same justice in other fields besides tragedy, including the epic itself.

2 (a8-10). Not all 'movement' is undesirable anyway, but only that which imitates low characters.

3 (a10-12). Tragedy can do without 'movement' (performance) entirely, just as the epic can.

4 (a14-16). Tragedy has everything the epic has, and music besides: an especially enjoyable feature.

5 (a17-18). It has vividness when read, as well as on the stage.

6 (a18-b12). It is more compact and unified, and therefore proportionately more enjoyable, than any epic.

7 (b12-15). It is better at performing the 'work' (the 'proper' or inherent pleasure) which is common to both genres.[8]

Besides the fourth counter-argument, whose significance in this context was previously established by Gottschlich, the only others which appear to be directly relevant to the task of assessing Lessing's proposition concerning the function of words in dramatic poetry are the third, fifth, and seventh. In view of the importance of determining the aesthetic goal of drama and the epic, it is best to defer discussion of the third and fifth counter-arguments until after the seventh has been adequately analyzed and the 'work' belonging to both genres properly identified.

Because of certain ambiguities in Aristotle's phraseology, however, the seventh counter-argument is perhaps the most difficult of all to interpret satisfactorily. The text of this troublesome item runs as follows: "If, then, tragedy is superior in all these respects and with respect to the function of art besides (for the two arts should produce, not any chance pleasure, but the one proper to them), it is evident that it must be superior, since it attains the goal more than the epic (does)."[9] Assessing the import of this passage, Else writes: "The last argument is, to our sorrow, not an argument but an allusion, and an unclear one at that. What *is* the '(previously) stated (pleasure)' which the two genres compete in producing?" (p. 651). Although he fully acknowledges the tentative nature of his conclusion, Else believes that Aristotle is referring to the statement which identifies the goal of tragedy as "the pleasure produced out of pity and fear by means of imitation" that was previously made in the opening section of the fourteenth chapter of the *Poetics*.[10] Accordingly, Else postulates that the same pleasure also constitutes the goal which Aristotle attributes to the epic poem.

Despite the fact that Aristotle's seventh counter-argument is not specifically mentioned in the correspondence between Lessing and Mendelssohn during the years 1756-57, an examination of the views expressed there strongly suggests that Lessing would not have concurred with Else's interpretation of this point. As part of his letter to Mendelssohn dated December 18, 1756, Lessing offers the possibility of an alternative interpretation of the seventh counter-argument by emphasizing the importance of Aristotle's contention that "one must not seek any and every kind of pleasure from tragedy, but the one proper to it." Oddly enough, this proposition is also taken from the same section in the fourteenth chapter of the *Poetics* from which Else draws support for his own interpretation of the seventh counter-argument. But in contrast to Else, who holds that Aristotle believed in a common goal for both tragic and epic poetry, Lessing takes the position that each of these genres has an end peculiar to itself which the poet must respect if he is to be a successful practitioner of his art. Considering the explicitness with which the Stagirite himself identifies the emotional response to be expected from tragedy, there can be little doubt that the evocation of pity and fear constitutes the formal objective of the tragic poet in terms of Aristotelean dramaturgy. In regard to the epic, however, it is far more difficult to determine the exact nature of the goal prescribed by Aristotle. Lessing, for his part, attempts to convince Mendelssohn that epic poetry is written to evoke feelings of admiration for the hero, rather than those of pity. Since the tragic and epic poets are actually working toward separate objectives, Lessing holds it essential to recognize that the relationship between plot and character differ markedly in each of these genres. By way of exemplification, he goes on to point out: "Der Heldendichter läßt seinen Helden unglücklich seyn, um seine Vollkommenheiten ins Licht zu setzen. Der Tragödienschreiber setzt seines Helden Vollkommenheiten ins Licht, um uns sein Unglück desto schmerzlicher zu machen" (XVII, 80). In all honesty, it must be acknowledged that Lessing offers no theoretical justification in his correspondence with Mendelssohn and Nicolai during these years to account for the fact that it has been a universal practice among poets over the centuries to select the admired hero as a subject for the epic and the pitied hero as a subject for the drama. More than a decade later, however, Lessing was to devote the seventy-seventh article of the *Hamburgische Dramaturgie* to a close examination of Aristotle's definition of tragedy and concludes on the basis of rigorous analysis that the evocation of pity and fear is the exclusive prerogative of dramatic poetry. Since he obviously rejects the idea of a common goal for both genres, Lessing would apparently be inclined to interpret Aristotle's seventh counter-argument to the effect that tragedy can arouse the emotions of pity and fear more effectively than the epic is able to evoke the sentiment of admiration.

Compared with the seventh, the third and fifth counter-arguments are far less intricate in character. An inspection of the actual language in which these propositions have been formulated would seem to admit of no other interpretation but that Aristotle is proclaiming the superiority of the dramatic genre to be wholly independent of theatrical performance. The text of the third counter-argument runs as follows: "Further, tragedy does its work even without movement (performance), like the epic; for it can convey its qualities through reading."[11] Similarly, the fifth states: " . . . and then it also has the element of vividness, in reading as well as in performance." Even though both of these propositions appear to be making essentially the same point, Else draws a vital distinction between them. While the third counter-argument merely establishes a parity between tragic and epic poetry with respect to their ability to dispense with performance, the fifth is more positive in nature in so far as it actually attributes a greater vividness to the dramatic than to the epic genre. Else's own restatement of the fifth counter-argument underscores the importance of this quality even more clearly than does the original and reads accordingly: "Tragedy (when properly composed) *has* 'vividness.' It is inherent in the dramatic method (δρώντων) and will communicate itself even to a reader, because it is written into the text, i.e., into the actions, feelings, etc., directly implied by the text. This is something the epic, as a narrative art, does not have inherently, although a poet like Homer may achieve it."[12] Thus the fifth counter-argument is the more important of the two, and it is the greater "vividness" of the dramatic method mentioned here that Lessing is seeking to explain on the basis of the theory of signs.

As far as an evaluation of the thesis advanced by Gottschlich is concerned, the third counter-argument is by no means unimportant and may be combined with the fifth for the purpose of demonstrating the untenability of his attempt to reduce Aristotle's position on the superiority of dramatic form to the theory of signs. Since the third counter-argument maintains that tragedy can dispense with performance and the fifth states that a play is able to communicate the quality of "vividness" in reading as well as in performance, the effects of spectacle (performance) and the music referred to in the fourth counter-argument may hardly be categorized as indispensable elements in Aristotle's concept of the dramatic method – much less, the source of its superiority. In view of Lessing's insistence that his own reason for maintaining the superiority of the drama is fully compatible with the doctrines set forth in the *Poetics*, it follows that any valid explanation of the process by which words in dramatic poetry are transformed into "natürliche Zeichen willkührlicher Dinge" must also be one which is completely independent of theatrical performance and the art of acting. Gottschlich's explanation, being based on the mimetic movements of the actor, may therefore be ruled out of consideration since it is contingent on the actual staging of a play. By the same token, one can also reject the feasibility of Gottschlich's attempt to equate the term "natürliche Zeichen willkührlicher Dinge" with the expression "natürliche Zeichen der Dinge" that was used in the fourth article of the *Dramaturgie* in reference to the mimetic gestures of the actor. Obviously, anyone who wishes to defend the validity of Gottschlich's exegesis must also be prepared to concede the existence of an irreconcilable contradiction between the arguments pertaining to the superiority of the drama presented in the *Poetics* and the one proposed in the letter to Nicolai despite Lessing's claim that these explanations are fully compatible.

Of course, it may be argued that if Gottschlich and other literary scholars could overlook the relevance of Aristotle's third and fifth counterarguments, it is equally possible for Lessing himself to have done so. To what extent then do Lessing's own writings indicate that he really took Aristotle's views concerning the function of theatrical performance into account and actually concurred with them? Evidence to the effect that he did *not* believe a play retained its "vividness" when merely read may be found in the foreword to his *Beyträge zur Historie und Aufnahme des Theaters*.[13] The significance of Lessing's arguments on this occasion is, however, vitiated by the fact that they are part of an early work published in 1750 – that is, many years before he could be considered wholly familiar with the contents of the *Poetics*. It was not until the autumn of 1756 that Lessing made a sustained effort to formulate a theory of tragedy and not until the early part of 1757 that he, stimulated by the publication of Nicolai's *Abhandlungen vom Trauerspiele* in the same year, undertook a study of Aristotle's treatise in the original Greek. Up to then, Lessing's knowledge of the *Poetics* was derived from the translations of Dacier and Curtius.[14]

An examination of Lessing's correspondence with Mendelssohn and Nicolai during the years 1756-57 will, moreover, confirm his full awareness of the significance of Aristotle's argument that the superiority of the dramatic genre is in no way dependent on its being staged. Lessing, in fact, explicitly adopts Aristotle's position as his own in the letter to Mendelssohn dated December 18, 1756. In reference to an exchange of ideas concerning the importance of illusion which Mendelssohn was then conducting with Nicolai, Lessing offers the following advice: "Wenn Sie Ihre Gedanken von der Illusion mit dem Hrn. Nicolai aufs Reine bringen werden, so vergessen Sie ja nicht, daß die ganze Lehre von der Illusion eigentlich den dramatischen Dichter nichts angeht, und die Vorstelling seines Stücks das Werk einer andern Kunst, als der Dichtkunst, ist. Das Trauerspiel muß auch ohne Vorstellung und Akteurs seine völlige Stärke behalten; und diese bey dem Leser zu äußern, braucht sie nicht mehr Illusion als jede andre Geschichte. Sehen Sie deswegen den Aristoteles noch gegen das Ende des 6ten und den Anfang des 14ten Hauptstücks nach" (XVII, 87-88). In both of the passages from the *Poetics* to which Lessing refers on this occasion, Aristotle actually anticipates the third and fifth counter-arguments that are set forth subsequently in the twenty-sixth chapter.

Since both passages mentioned in the letter to Mendelssohn are highly germane to the problem of establishing Lessing's own position concerning the function of theatrical performance, each needs to be considered in full. Viewed jointly, these items really constitute a single extended argument on the superfluity of the type of illusion produced through the effects of costuming and staging. Within the sixth chapter, for example, Aristotle breaks up the concept of tragedy into six constituent parts – visual appearance, character, plot, speech, song, and thought – and analyzes each part in order of relative importance. Visual appearance, in keeping with the low prestige accorded it, is reserved until the end of the chapter for discussion and receives the following assessment: "As for the costuming, it has emotional power to be sure, but is the least artistic element, the least integral to the art of poetry; for the capacity of the tragic art exists even without a competition or actors, and moreover in the execution of the masks and costumes the costumer's art plays a more decisive role than the art of the poets."[15] Resuming this argument once again in chapter fourteen, Aristotle declares:

> Now it is possible for the fearful and pathetic effect to come from the costuming; but it is

also possible for it to come from the structure of events itself, which is theoretically prior and the mark of a better poet. For even without seeing a play, the plot should be so constructed that anyone who hears the events as they unfold will both shudder and be moved to pity at the outcome: which is what one would feel at hearing the plot of *Oedipus*. The attempt to produce this effect through the costuming is less artistic and something which requires the services of a choregus.* But those who try to produce through the costuming not the effect of fear but merely that of the monstrous, have nothing in common with tragedy at all. For one must not seek any and every kind of pleasure from tragedy, but the one proper to it. And since it is the pleasure that comes from pity and fear by means of imitation which the poet should try to produce, it is clear that this must be built into the plot.[16]

Although the passages from the *Poetics* mentioned by Lessing in his letter to Mendelssohn are never identified by section or line number, the above citations are probably extensive enough to contain all that he wished to call to his friend's attention at the time. In view of the unreservedly Aristotelian character of his advice to Mendelssohn on this occasion, there remains little doubt as to Lessing's own conviction that the pre-eminence

* The choregus was the one who defrayed the cost of the performance.

of the dramatic genre is not essentially a function of theatrical performance. Consequently, the superiority which the drama enjoys by virtue of its ability to transform words into "natural signs of arbitrary objects" cannot be legitimately explained on the basis of the scenery, the costuming, the gestures and facial expressions of the actor, or any other effect of staging, but must be attributed solely to qualities which are inherent in its written form.[17]

V. THE NATURE OF ILLUSION

Viewed in the light of Lessing's subsequent assertions on dramatic theory, the content of the previously-cited letter to Mendelssohn appears somewhat paradoxical. On the one hand, the idea that theatrical performance is not an essential part of the dramatic method was to remain a permanent aspect of his critical system. On the other, his position in regard to the importance of illusion seems to have undergone considerable revision in his later thinking. Both in *Laokoon* and in the *Hamburgische Dramaturgie*, for example, he repeatedly stresses the necessity for its presence. His main objective in writing *Laokoon*, it may be argued, was to demonstrate that description by the technique of enumerating coexistent parts precludes the establishment of illusion. In the eleventh article of the *Dramaturgie*, furthermore, he explicitly states that the goal of a dramatist should be the creation of illusion, for without it, he reasons, it is impossible to arouse sympathy on the part of the spectator (IX, 228). And it follows that without sympathy, there would be no catharsis and tragedy would then fail to attain its proper end. The very prominence which Lessing subsequently assigns to the concept of illusion (which he variously renders by the words *Illusion* or *Täuschung*) contrasts strangely with his earlier comment belittling its importance.[1]

In the work entitled *Lessing's Dramatic Theory*, John George Robertson attempts to resolve the discrepancy between the views which Lessing expressed in his early letters to Mendelssohn and Nicolai and those to be found in the critical writings of his maturity. As part of his explanation, Robertson observes: "In the period of his correspondence with Mendelssohn and Nicolai on tragedy he [Lessing] had refused to countenance the idea that illusion is essential to the aesthetic effect... But by the time he came to write *Laokoon*, where he had necessarily much to say on illusion, he had thought more deeply on the subject; and in the *Dramaturgie* he has plainly accepted Mendelssohn's views. In the passages [of the *Dramaturgie*] where he discusses or refers to illusion, there is no essential disparity between his standpoint and that of his friend."[2] Robertson's solution to the problem, however, may be deemed unsatisfactory for several important reasons. To begin with, it fails to take into consideration that Mendelssohn's own concept of illusion evolved only gradually over a period of many years and that his numerous writings on the topic are not in themselves fully consistent as to content.[3] It is therefore misleading to speak of "Mendelssohn's views" as though they comprise a single, unified doctrine. Robertson, moreover, leaves his readers with the distinct impression that Lessing subsequently came to accept the ideas concerning the nature of illusion which Mendelssohn espoused during the course of their 1756-57 correspondence – an interpretation which vastly oversimplifies a far more complex situation. In order to be able to appreciate the changes which occurred in Lessing's thinking on the subject of illusion, his reactions to Mendelssohn's initial proposals in this area need to be described in detail.

The topic itself was first broached by Mendelssohn in his letter to Lessing dated November 23, 1756. After evaluating most of the contents from an earlier letter by Lessing on the nature of tragedy, Mendelssohn asks to be excused from discussing several concepts which are highly pertinent to their inquiry until after he has had a chance to consult with Nicolai. "Meine Gedanken vom Schrecken und vom Weinen kann ich Ihnen nicht eher eröfnen," he informs Lessing, "bis ich mich mit unserm Hrn. Nicolai darüber besprochen habe... Ueber alles dieses wollen wir [Nicolai and he] uns weitläufiger heraus lassen, wenn wir erst unsere Gedanken von der Wirkung der theatralischen Illusion... in Ordnung gebracht haben" (XIX, 51). Several weeks later in a letter to Mendelssohn dated December 18, 1756, Lessing offers his friend the advice concerning illusion that was cited above in connection with the previous discussion on Aristotle and the necessity for theatrical performance. In this letter, it may be recalled, the concept of illusion was dismissed by Lessing as being totally irrelevant in regard to questions involving the literary merits of a dramatic work. Here too, in support of his contention that a tragedy "muß auch ohne Vorstellung und Akteurs seine völlige Stärke behalten," Lessing refers Mendelssohn to the arguments concerning the superfluity of the effects of costuming and staging that are set forth by Aristotle at the end of the sixth and at the opening of the fourteenth chapters of the *Poetics*.

In a subsequent letter written sometime during January 1757, Mendelssohn responds directly to his friend's suggestions by asserting: "Was ich für einen Begriff mit dem Worte Illusion verknüpfe, werden Sie aus beykommenden Blättern ersehen. Im 14ten Hauptstück vom Aristoteles finde ich nichts, das meinen Lehrsätzen widerspricht... und wenn ich dem Worte *Illusion* nicht den Verstand gegeben, den es nach dem Sprachgebrauch haben sollte, so streichen Sie es immer durch, und setzen ein anderes Zeichen dafür hin" (XIX, 65). Lessing, however, rules out the possibility of semantic disagreement. "Ueber das Wort," he assures Mendelssohn in his letter of February 2, 1757, "werde ich Ihnen keine Schwierigkeiten machen" (XVII, 90). To judge from the correspondence written by the two men during this period, the term is being used conventionally in reference to the type of aesthetic experience that is sufficiently true to life as to be virtually indistinguishable from reality.[4] Even though he fully agrees with Mendelssohn on the meaning of the term, Lessing, for his part, is simply unable to accept the idea that it is possible for any form of art to attain this degree of verisimilitude. Having apparently committed himself to the Abbé Dubos' position that imitation can never be as forceful as nature itself, he is unwilling to concede that a person contemplating a painting or attending a theatrical performance is ever deceived to the point of believing that he is experiencing reality rather than art.[5] Although Mendelssohn himself believes that art has the power to deceive completely, the theory of illusion that he attempts to formulate in the course of these discussions is a remarkably subtle one.

Rather than peruse the scattered pronouncements concerning the nature of illusion that Mendelssohn makes in his correspondence during the years 1756-57, it is best to study these ideas in the form in which they are presented in his treatise *Von der Herrschaft über die Neigungen*. Produced under the direct stimulus of his exchange of ideas with Lessing and Nicolai, this work was completed by the early summer of 1757 and amounts to a summary of the position which he took at that time. In the section entitled "Von der Illusion," Mendelssohn utilizes the popularly-held epistemological distinction between the upper (rational) and the lower (sensual) faculties of the soul for the purpose of explaining the nature of what he terms "aesthetic illusion." The sense impressions communicated by a work of art, he maintains, initially affect the lower faculties of the soul in the same manner as would those of its counterpart in real life. In order for a work of art to be successful, the lower faculties of the soul must at first be completely convinced of the sensual reality of the objects or actions depicted. The activity of the higher or rational faculties, however, intervenes before long and reminds us that what is being experienced is only an imitation of reality. Far from deploring this intervention, Mendelssohn holds that the interplay between the higher and the lower faculties of the soul is essential to aesthetic enjoyment. As long as man's senses are under the domination of illusion, art is confounded with reality. Only through the judgment of the rational faculties is man able to appreciate the fact that the vividness of the sense impressions and emotions communicated through an aesthetic medium have been achieved by means of the imitative powers of art. It is therefore necessary that the higher faculties of the soul make a comparison between the imitation of nature embodied in a work of art and the archetype in reality which corresponds to it. Mendelssohn chooses to designate this interplay between sense perception and the faculty of judgment as "aesthetic illusion" in order to convey the idea that a conscious recognition of the difference between art and reality is an indispensable part of every aesthetic experience. Although this argument may appear to have a greater relevance for the plastic arts than for poetry, Mendelssohn states at the very outset of "Von der Illusion" that he considers his theory to be equally valid for all varieties of literary expression as well. "Der Dichter muß vollkommen sinnlich reden," he declares, "daher müssen uns alle seine Reden ästhetisch illudiren."[6]

Mendelssohn believes that the interplay between sense perception and the faculty of judgment may be best substantiated through an analysis of man's aesthetic response to works depicting the type of objects and actions which would evoke unpleasant emotions had they actually been encountered in reality. In this context, he makes an attempt to improve upon the explanation reputedly offered by Aristotle to account for the pleasure which humans have always taken in works of imitation. As recounted by Mendelssohn in the concluding section of "Von der Illusion," Aristotle contends a man who unexpectedly comes across a painting of a snake will attach a value to the picture which is in direct proportion to the amount of fear that was originally induced by it. The subsequent pleasure taken in the imitation is, Aristotle reportedly argues, the result of the spectactor's sense of relief at being freed from an imagined danger. Actually, the argument purported to have been made by the Stagirite was most likely derived from the opening lines in the third section of Nicolas Boileau's *L'Art poétique*. Here Boileau writes:

Il n'est point de Serpent, ni de Monstre odieux,
Qui par l'Art imité ne puisse plaire aux yeux.
D'un pinceau delicat l'artifice agreable
Du plus affreux objet fait un objet aimable.

The passage in the *Poetics* which most closely parallels Boileau's thoughts on the matter is probably the section in the fourth chapter where Aristotle asserts: "Imitation is a part of men's nature from childhood... There are things we find painful to look at themselves, but of which we view the most accurate reproductions with pleasure: for example, replicas of the most unprepossessing animals, or of cadavers" (1448b, 5-12). Irrespective of its true provenience, however, Mendelssohn categorically rejects the idea that the spectator's sense of relief is the source of the subsequent pleasure taken in the picture of the snake. In his counter-explanation, he takes the position that the initial fear simply functions, in retrospect, as a criterion which serves to corroborate the fact that the artist has succeeded in creating a convincing imitation of nature.

In the letter to Mendelssohn dated February 2, 1757, Lessing offers his most detailed criticism of the theory of aesthetic illusion and devotes several paragraphs of this letter to an analysis of the argument concerning the picture of the snake. For the sake of demonstrating that the aesthetic effect created by the picture of the snake may be explained without recourse to the concept of illusion, Lessing asks Mendelssohn to consider an analogous situation in which the imitation in question is the painting of a beautiful woman rather than that of an unpleasant object. On the basis of Mendelssohn's thesis, the viewer's pleasure should increase upon suddenly discovering that the beautiful image before him is not a real woman at all, but actually the work of an artist. Lessing, for his part, believes that under these circumstances the viewer would be much more inclined to react with vexation at the thought of such perfection physically eluding him. Since a total deception of the senses would seem to be undesirable in connection with a picture of a beautiful woman, it follows that complete illusion should be equally superfluous in the case of a painted snake. In general, therefore, it is entirely unnecessary to postulate an initial state of illusion in which art and reality are indistinguishable.[7] Eschewing any interplay between the higher and lower faculties of the soul, Lessing holds that aesthetic experience is homogeneous and that the deception of the senses effected through the agency of art is always self-conscious and playful. His point of view is thus substantially the same as that of Dubos.

Lessing's argument against the theory of aesthetic illusion did not remain unheeded. The influence of this criticism is readily apparent from the manner in which Mendelssohn reformulates his position in a treatise first published in 1761 entitled *Rhapsodie, oder Zusätze zu den Briefen über die Empfindungen*. Here he maintains that the reason why even the most frightful events may be depicted in the plastic arts and on the stage without becoming offensive is due to the fact that the viewer himself implicitly recognizes the imitative status of aesthetic experience. There are still moments, Mendelssohn concedes, when a person may get carried away and attribute a natural existence to the signs employed for the purpose of imitating reality. "Allein dieser Zauber dauert so lange," he now argues, "als nöthig ist, unserm Begriffe von dem Gegenstande das gehörige Leben und Feuer zu geben."[8] In any case, this self-imposed state of deception is a tenuous condition which requires an exertion of the will in order for it to be sustained. It may, furthermore, be disrupted whenever the experience threatens to become unpleasant by simply withdrawing the mental energy needed to suppress one's awareness of those attributes which tend to identify the work of art as an imitation. The resulting consciousness of details like the texture of an artist's canvas or the marble surface of a statue is a sufficient reminder that one is not in the presence of reality, but of an imitation.

Mendelssohn goes on to point out that even under normal circumstances, an awareness of such qualities is not without advantage. The total absence of these tell-tale signs of imitation would, for example, surely induce a state of uneasiness or repulsion on the part of the viewer. As a case in point, he mentions the unpleasant feelings which are occasioned whenever synthetic columns or wax statues are too life-like. In making this observation, however, Mendelssohn does not mean to imply that an artist should deliberately seek to emphasize the artificiality of his creations in order to preclude the possibility of complete illusion. There is actually no need to do so, and artists are, in fact, exhorted quite to the contrary. "Die Kunst muss alle Kräfte des Genies aufbieten," Mendelssohn insists, "die Nachahmung und die dadurch zu erhaltende Täuschung vollkommen zu machen, und sie kann es sicher den zufälligen Umständen, der Auszierung, dem Orte, der Materie und tausend andern, nicht unter dem Gebiete der Kunst stehenden Nebendingen überlassen, der Seele die nöthige Erinnerung zu geben, dass sie Kunst und nicht Natur vor sich habe" (II, 108).

If the ideas which Mendelssohn advocated in "Von der Illusion" are compared with the later and maturer views to be found in his *Rhapsodie*, it is clear that he has done much to overcome the most objectionable features of his earlier theory. Underscoring the vastly improved nature of the subsequent formulation, Ludwig Goldstein remarks:

Zweifellos ist nich nur die Form, in die sich die Theorie in dem vorstehenden Stücke kleidet, weit annehmbarer als bisher, sondern sie hat auch selbst an Klarheit und Durchsichtigkeit gewonnen. Ihr Vertreter ist sich selbst bewußt geworden, daß ein wahres Kunstwerk nie solcher Merkmale entbehren darf, die es von vornherein als ein Werk der Nachahmung bezeichnen, und er würde jetzt jedenfalls das irreleitende Beispiel von der gemalten Schlange, als Beleg für seine Ideen, selbst von der Hand gewiesen haben.
... Diese Erkenntnis war von Anfang an richtig vorbereitet und im §12 des Aufsatzes "Von der Herrschaft über die Neigungen" bereits theoretisch ausgesprochen, ist dann aber durch

ungeeignete Exemplifikation getrübt und verdunkelt worden bis sie endlich in der "Rhapsodie" am reinsten zum Ausdruck gelangt.[9]

In effecting the aforementioned revisions of his earlier theory, Mendelssohn has come extremely close to accepting the proposition that aesthetic experience does not require a total deception of the senses.

Considering the manner in which Mendelssohn has modified the meaning traditionally associated with the concept of illusion, Lessing's use of the term in the critical writings of his maturity may be easily reconciled with his former depreciation of its aesthetic significance during the years 1756-57. Basically, his refusal to accept the principle of illusion at that time must be attributed to an intuitive psychological dissatisfaction with the idea that the success of a painting or theatrical performance is contingent on its capacity to induce a state of total deception in the mind of the spectator. In view of the extent to which Mendelssohn has mitigated this aspect of his theory in the *Rhapsodie*, the concept of illusion becomes increasingly feasible to Lessing as a criterion of aesthetic excellence. At some point in his thinking, furthermore, Lessing has apparently come to equate the term "illusion" with the quality of "vividness" which Aristotle alludes to on several occasions in the *Poetics*.[10] As a result of this semantic shift, it is now possible for Lessing to employ the term "illusion" in reference to the aesthetic qualities which are communicated through the dialogue of a play by virtue of its written form alone.[11] Even when Lessing refers to the effects of illusion in connection with dramatic performances on the stage, it is not his intention to imply that the audience has somehow been rendered oblivious to the imitative status of theatrical experience. Indeed, he by no means rules out the possibility that a full awareness of the audience's presence might actually serve to promote a greater emotional responsiveness on the part of the individual spectator himself. In the eighty-first *Literaturbrief*, for example, Lessing warmly endorses the observation that Diderot makes in a postscript to his play *Le Fils naturel* in regard to the manner in which the vast number of spectators in attendance at Greek and Roman theaters must have intensified the effectiveness of a dramatic performance.[12] Notwithstanding the fact that the concept of "vividness" or "illusion" is relevant to all forms of literature, both Aristotle and Lessing are in full agreement that the aesthetic values implied thereby are most successfully achieved through the medium of drama.

VI. THE SUPERIORITY OF THE DRAMA

Supplementing the argument of the *Poetics*, Lessing contends that the greater "vividness" or "illusion" manifested in the drama should be viewed as a function of the theory of signs. In order to be able to isolate the factors which permit words in a play to become "natural signs of arbitrary objects," the difference between the dramatic and epic genres needs to be analyzed in terms of their aesthetic effect. One of the best indications of Lessing's views on the matter may be found in his letter to Heinrich Wilhelm Gerstenberg dated February 25, 1768. In the course of this letter, Lessing offers a critical evaluation of *Ugolino*, a play which Gerstenberg based on a passage in Dante's *Divine Comedy*. "Es ist mir lieb," he informs the author, "Ihren Ugolino einmal gelesen zu haben, nehmlich in der Absicht mich der Täuschung zu überlaßen: zum zweytenmale lese ich ihn *in dieser Absicht* gewiß nicht wieder. Woher dieses?"[1] In answer to this query, Lessing proceeds to ascribe his own general dissatisfaction with *Ugolino* to the fact that there is entirely too much unmerited suffering in the play. Even the troubles of the sole person in it who may be said to bear a tragic guilt are, he believes, incommensurate with his actual fault. As a result, the torments to which the protagonists are subjected during the course of the action are unbearably painful to the reader or spectator. In anticipation of a possible rejoinder from Gerstenberg to the effect that this criticism would apply equally to Dante, Lessing raises the issue himself and goes on to deny its relevance by means of the following argument: "Nein: Bey dem Dante hören wir die Geschichte als *geschehen:* bey Ihnen sehn wir sie als *geschehend.* Es ist ganz etwas anders, ob ich das Schreckliche hinter mir, oder vor mir erblicke. Ganz etwas anders, ob ich höre, durch dieses Elend kam der Held durch, das überstand er: oder ich sehe, durch dieses soll er durch, dieses soll er überstehen."[2] For this reason, he then concludes: "Der Unterschied der Gattung macht hier alles." To judge from these remarks concerning *Ugolino,* Lessing appears to be convinced that the greater efficacy of dramatic form should be attributed to its unique ability to simulate the quality of present time.

In the process of explaining her own theory of genre in *Die Logik der Dichtung,* Käthe Hamburger seriously contests the validity of distinguishing between the dramatic and epic forms on a temporal basis. The essence of her objection consists in the thesis that the preterite as employed in epic narration loses its normal grammatical function of designating past time.[3] This argument should not, however, be construed as a claim on her part that a reader experiences the events described in an epic form like the novel as though they were actually occurring in the present, but rather that the temporal perspective established by all literary genres is of a purely fictive, timeless quality which has little to do with real time (pp. 78-84). Miss Hamburger makes this point most forcefully in taking issue with certain remarks of Thornton Wilder concerning the temporal effect fo the dramatic genre.[4] "Nicht nur auf der Bühne, wie Thornton Wilder meint," she observes, "sondern auch im Roman, im Epos ist es immer 'jetzt' – nur daß wir es dort wahrnehmend, hier vorstellend erleben, nicht kraft der Anschauung sondern kraft der Anschaulichkeit" (p. 172). Since both the drama's depiction of present action and the epic's narration of past events are equally fictive, Miss Hamburger sees little difference in the temporal effect of the two genres – not even under the circumstances where a play is actually performed on stage, rather than simply read in private. As a case in point, she takes the performance of *Miss Sara Sampson* which is described in the thirteenth article of the *Hamburgische Dramaturgie*. After commenting on the actual physical presence of Lessing as a spectator sitting in the audience and of Sophie Friederike Hensel as an actress playing the title role at that performance, Miss Hamburger introduces an important distinction with respect to Madame Hensel's own existence and that of the character she is portraying on stage by declaring:

> Aber Mellefonts Zimmer im Gasthaus, in das Sara eintritt, diese selbst, Mellefont und die übrigen Personen existieren in keiner realeren Gegenwart oder Gegenwärtigkeit, als sie in der Form von Romanpersonen existieren würden. Analysieren wir unser Erlebnis im Theater ge-

THE SUPERIORITY OF THE DRAMA

nauer, so bemerken wir, daß wir uns dort ebensogut wie in einer Lesesituation bewußt sind, daß das reale Hier und Jetzt der Bühne, und damit unser Hier und Jetzt im Zuschauerraum, nicht identisch mit dem fiktiven Hier und Jetzt der Dramenhandlung ist. Lebend in der sich abspielenden Handlung vergessen wir der Bühne als Bühne ebenso wie wir der Vergangenheitsform der erzählenden Verben, ja radikal gesprochen des Erzählens selbst vergessen.[5]

Since she sees little difference in the fictive quality communicated by a drama that is performed and an epic that is read, it is not surprising to find that Miss Hamburger uses the term "illusion" in reference to both experiences.

In place of a temporal distinction between the two genres, Miss Hamburger proposes to separate the dramatic from the epic method on the basis of a factor which she identifies as "the narrative function" (*Erzählfunktion*), the magnitude of which is simply a measure of the reader's awareness of the narrator's presence in a fictional work and of his role in the process of narration. In drama, she maintains, the narrative function is reduced to zero and the reader or playgoer is not conscious of the author, but solely of the interactions of the characters themselves (p. 158). Even though the narrative function of the poet can never be entirely eliminated from epic poetry, it would be incorrect to infer that Miss Hamburger regards the epic as a subjective form of art. While conceding that the mediation of a narrator makes the epic more subjective than the drama (pp. 118-119), she defends the basic objectivity of the epic technique by insisting: "Er [der erzählende Dichter] ist es, der erzählt, aber er erzählt nicht *von* seinen Gestalten, sondern er erzählt *die* Gestalten."[6] Of course, this characterization of narrative fiction does not apply to novels written in the first person. Such works are inextricably associated with the subjective impressions of a particular individual (*Ich-origo*) as opposed to the seemingly objective assertions made about the world by the anonymous commentator of the epic poem and impersonal novel (p. 249).

In the analysis of the epic and dramatic techniques set forth in the *Poetics*, Aristotle himself attaches a major significance to the narrative function as a structural criterion and appears to derive the superiority of the drama primarily from the fact that it is able to dispense with narration entirely. He even holds that a reduction in the role of the narrator is advantageous in the epic itself and bestows much praise on Homer for his extensive use of the dramatic method. Stressing the importance of the dramatic element in Homer's poems, Aristotle remarks:

> Homer deserves our admiration for many reasons, but particularly because he alone of the (epic) poets is not unaware what it is one should be composing himself. Namely, the

poet himself ought to do as little talking as possible; for it is not by virtue of that that he he is a poet. Now the others are on stage themselves, in competition, the whole time, and imitate but little and occasionally, whereas he, after a few words by way of preface, immediately brings on stage a man or a woman or some other character, and not one characterless but (all) having character.[7]

It is undoubtedly the reduction of the narrative function described here which is uppermost in Lessing's mind when he observes in his letter to Nicolai: "Daß die dramatische Poesie die höchste, ja die einzige Poesie ist, hat schon Aristoteles gesagt, und er giebt der Epopee nur in so fern die zweyte Stelle, als sie größten Theils dramatisch ist, oder seyn kann."[8]

Lessing, moreover, appears to be convinced that the elimination of the narrative function and the quality of present time are by no means mutually exclusive attributes. A temporal distinction between the dramatic and epic genres is, he believes, already implicit in the definition of tragedy which was formally stated in the sixth chapter of the *Poetics*. In the seventy-seventh article of the *Hamburgische Dramaturgie*, Lessing translates this renowned passage as follows: "'Die Tragödie, sagt er [Aristotle], ist die Nachahmung einer Handlung, ... die nicht vermittelst der Erzehlung, sondern vermittelst des Mitleids und der Furcht, die Reinigung dieser und dergleichen Leidenschaften bewirket.'"⁹ Lessing then goes on to remark: "Wem sollte hier nicht der sonderbare Gegensatz, 'nicht vermittelst der Erzehlung, sondern vermittelst des Mitleids und der Furcht,' befremden? ... Scheinet hier also Aristoteles nicht einen Sprung zu machen? Scheinet hier nicht offenbar der eigentliche Gegensatz der Erzehlung, welches die dramatische Form ist, zu fehlen?"¹⁰ As a solution to the problem posed by this discrepancy, Lessing offers an explanation which is based on the proposition that the emotions of pity and fear can be induced *only* by means of the dramatic and *never* by the narrative form – at least to the degree necessary to effect a catharsis of these emotions. In attributing this aesthetic thesis to Aristotle, Lessing argues: "Kurz, die Sache ist diese: Aristoteles bemerkte, daß das Mitleid nothwendig ein vorhandenes Uebel erfodere; daß wir längst vergangene oder fern in der Zukunft bevorstehende Uebel entweder gar nicht, oder doch bey weitem nicht so stark bemitleiden können, als ein anwesendes; daß es folglich nothwendig sey, die Handlung, durch welche wir Mitleid erregen wollen, nicht als vergangen, das ist, in der erzehlenden Form, sondern als gegenwärtig, das ist, in der dramatischen Form, nachzuahmen."¹¹ Since pity and fear can only be aroused by an action presented in dramatic form, Lessing holds that it really makes little difference if the *end* is substituted for the *means* indispensable for its attainment. Aristotle's leap in thought is, accordingly, merely the result of his desire for brevity on this occasion. Even if one does not choose to accept Lessing's analysis in its entirety, there is little reason to doubt that a temporal distinction between the dramatic and epic genres constitutes an integral part of the definition of tragedy set forth in the sixth chapter of the *Poetics*. In terms of Aristotelean dramaturgy, therefore, the elimination of the narrative function and the quality of present time are not alternative explanations of the dramatic method, as they seem to be for Miss Hamburger, but rather are mutually dependent attributes – the one of necessity implying the other. Because of the simultaneous operation of these two factors, it becomes possible for tragedy to evoke the degree of illusion that is necessary in order to arouse pity and fear on the part of the spectator.

Despite the fact that Lessing fully concurs with the assessment of the dramatic and epic genres set forth in the *Poetics*, he is not altogether satisfied with the manner in which Aristotle has formulated his arguments. It may be recalled that Lessing informed Nicolai of certain apprehensions concerning the Stagirite's position on the superiority of the dramatic method and suggested the possibility of its improvement by asserting: "Der Grund, den er [Aristotle] davon angiebt, ist zwar nicht der meinige; aber er läßt sich auf meinen reduciren, und wird nur durch diese Reduction auf meinen, vor aller falschen Anwendung gesichert." If one were to seek an area in which Aristotle's delineation of dramatic technique is most subject to misunderstanding, it would appear to lie in the possible distortion of his views concerning the elimination of the narrative function. Strictly interpreted, this dictum might, for example, result in condemning the legitimate use of narration within the context of a dramatic action by the characters themselves. As a case in point, one need only consider the narrative exposition of Boccaccio's ring parable in Lessing's own play *Nathan der Weise*. With respect to the manner in which the narrative form of the ring parable has prevented its dramatic function from being duly appreciated, Stuart Atkins points out:

> As a result, there has evolved a tendency to regard the dramatic poem *Nathan der Weise* as a sort of ring whose only *raison d'être* is to furnish a setting for the precious stone which is the famous parable, or else a tendency to regard the parable of the rings as an independent text properly printed as such in anthologies of German verse. In view of the fact that the creator of *Nathan der Weise* was a skillful and successful dramatist several of whose works – *Nathan* included – still hold the stage, the former tendency cannot be plausibly justified. And the latter tendency uncritically ignores two incontrovertible points: (1) that the ring parable is actually a discontinuous text in a larger dramatic context; (2) that in such a context the ring parable demands to be read

as dramatic statement – for instance, as revelation of character in action.[12]

After discussing the circumstances surrounding the telling of the ring parable and its place within the framework of the play as a whole, Atkins underscores the dramatic nature of *Nathan der Weise* by declaring: "As author of *Pope ein Metaphysiker!* and the *Hamburg Dramaturgy*, Lessing well knew that drama is character in action, not philosophic statement; it can only present, *as action*, life as it is, might be, or should be" (p. 266).

In the fifty-third article of the *Hamburgische Dramaturgie*, Lessing himself argues the same point in objecting to a remark by Voltaire concerning Molière's *L'École des femmes*. Citing his French contemporary directly, Lessing reports: "'Die Frauenschule, sagt der Herr von Voltaire, war ein Stück von einer ganz neuen Gattung, worinn zwar alles nur Erzehlung, aber doch so künstliche Erzehlung ist, daß alles Handlung zu seyn scheinet'" (X, 6). Although Lessing is by no means unalterably opposed to a mixing of the genres, he nevertheless views the use of narration as a substitute for dramatic action on stage with pronounced disfavor.[13] This is made abundantly clear on several occasions in the *Dramaturgie*. In the ninth article, for example Lessing takes exception to a playwright's attempt to establish the goodness of his hero by means of the testimony of others. "Wir wollen es auf der Bühne sehen," he insists, "wer die Menschen sind, und können es nur aus ihren Thaten sehen" (IX, 219). Similarly with respect to Voltaire's assessment of the technique used in *L'École des femmes,* Lessing observes: "Mehr oder weniger künstlich, Erzehlung bleibt immer Erzehlung, und wir wollen auf dem Theater wirkliche Handlungen sehen" (X, 6). Continuing this argument, he goes on to point out that the narrative passages in Molière's play function in such a way as to reveal the character of either the speaker himself or the persons attending his speech. On these grounds, Lessing concludes: "Also, anstatt von der Frauenschule zu sagen, daß alles darinn Handlung scheine, obgleich alles nur Erzehlung sey, glaubte ich mit mehrerm Rechte sagen zu können, daß alles Handlung darinn sey, obgleich alles nur Erzehlung zu seyn scheine" (X, 7).

It is apparently to avoid the type of problem which besets Voltaire on this occasion that Lessing proposes to reformulate the dramatic method in terms of the theory of signs. Generally speaking, a natural sign is one which shares in the attributes belonging to the model being imitated. Since words in a dramatic dialogue are used in imitation of human discourse, they may properly be deemed "natural signs of arbitrary objects." Nonetheless, it is difficult to see how this formulation can be related to questions concerning the role of narration in drama. Clearly, Lessing must have introduced a refinement into the concept of natural signs which goes beyond the formal statements of either Dubos or Mendelssohn. A good indication of what Lessing has in mind may be found in the notes for the continuation of *Laokoon* that were written sometime during the spring or summer of 1766. Here, in regard to the use of natural signs in painting, the artist is given the following advice:

> Und hiernächst laße man sich belehren, daß selbst ihre natürlichen Zeichen unter gewißen Umständen, es völlige zu seyn aufhören können.
> Ich meine nehmlich so: unter diesen natürlichen Zeichen sind die vornehmsten, Linien, und aus diesen zusammengesetzte Figuren. Nun ist es aber nicht genug, daß diese Linien unter sich eben das Verhältniß haben, welches sie in der Natur haben; eine jede derselben muß auch die nehmliche, und nicht bloß verjüngte Dimension haben, die sie in der Natur hat, oder in demjenigen Gesichtspunkte haben würde, aus welchem das Gemählde betrachtet werden soll.
> Derjenige Mahler also, welcher sich vollkommen natürlicher Zeichen bedienen will, muß in Lebensgröße, oder wenigstens nicht merklich unter Lebensgröße mahlen. (XIV, 423)

In brief, artists are urged to employ spatial relations which are close to life size so as to avoid the loss of illusion that comes about as a consequence of working with reduced dimensions. Unfortunately, Lessing does not offer any similar instruction concerning the proper use of natural signs in dramatic discourse. It is perfectly feasible, however, to construct an analogous argument pertaining to dramatic poetry on the basis of the advice which Lessing gives to the painter on this occasion. If a work of art employing form and color in space ought to imitate objects in life size, it also follows that a work of dramatic literature employing articulated sounds in time should imitate actions in present time. Unless the dialogue in a play is contemporaneous with the dramatic action, the playwright is not really using words in the manner of natural signs. As a consequence of this temporal criterion, the use of narration is restricted to those contexts in which it simultaneously serves to reveal character in action. Only in this way is it possible for narrative passages to be made an integral part of dramatic action and for the words in them to attain the status of "natural signs of arbitrary objects." By virtue of this reformulation of the dramatic method, Lessing believes that Aristotle's position on narration can be protected from distortion without in any way jeopardizing the unique capacity of the drama to simulate the quality of present time.

Of course, the cogency of this emendation to the *Poetics* depends largely on one's willingness to accept the temporal distinction which Lessing draws between the epic and the drama. Interestingly enough, Goethe and Schiller are frequently credited with having been the first to distinguish between these two genres on a temporal basis.

The cause of this misconception may in all likelihood be attributed to Schiller's letter to Wilhelm von Humboldt dated June 27, 1798. Here Schiller asserts: "Goethe und ich haben uns epische und dramatische Poesie auf eine einfachere Art unterschieden, als Ihr Weg Ihnen erlaubte, und diesen Unterschied überhaupt nicht so groß gefunden... Uns scheint, daß Epopöe und Tragödie durch nichts als durch die vergangene und die gegenwärtige Zeit sich unterscheiden."[14] However, it should be noted that a similar temporal distinction between the epic and the drama was already formulated in articles seventy-seven and eighty of the *Hamburgische Dramaturgie* – that is, long before Goethe and Schiller ever had occasion to exchange views on the topic. Although no idea of this type can be entirely without precedent, it is Lessing who deserves recognition as the one primarily responsible for introducing a temporal factor into discussions concerning the nature of the various literary genres.

Over the past few decades, the theory of genre has received an unusual amount of attention from contemporary literary theorists and historians. In Germany, much of this attention has been directed toward a reexamination of the theory of genre in the eighteenth century. As a result, two critical treatises have emerged from relative obscurity and are now duly appreciated for their importance in regard to the problem of narration; namely, *Über Handlung, Gespräch und Erzählung* by Johann Jakob Engel and *Versuch über den*

Roman by Friedrich von Blanckenburg.[15] In these works, each of which was first published in 1774, Aristotle's position on the superiority of the drama is disregarded and aesthetic parity bestowed to the category of the novel. Neither author, however, finds it necessary to take issue with the temporal distinction between the epic and the drama proposed by Lessing. They simply contend that the novel is a superior vehicle for the presentation of character and the depiction of mental processes. Although Lessing was undoubtedly familiar with the arguments advanced by Engel and Blanckenburg, there is no evidence to indicate that he ever felt any obligation to modify his belief in the pre-eminence of the dramatic genre.

VII. POETRY AS A MIMETIC ART

Anyone who wishes to appreciate the full scope of Lessing's aesthetic philosophy must ultimately come to terms with the concept of imitation. Like most critics of the eighteenth century, Lessing subscribed to the principle that art is an endeavor to imitate nature.[1] Although such eminent writers of antiquity as Plato, Horace, Longinus, and Quintilian had also made extensive use of the concept of imitation, the principle has come to be most closely associated with Aristotle ever since the rediscovery of the *Poetics* during the late Renaissance. Nowhere in the *Poetics* or any of his other writings, however, does Aristotle actually define the meaning of the term "imitation." So as to establish Aristotle's position on imitation as quickly as possible, it will prove advantageous to turn to Jean H. Hagstrum's book entitled *The Sister Arts*. In it, the author provides a brief restatement of Aristotle's position that runs as follows: "For Aristotle imitation meant doing in another realm what nature does in hers: the achievement in matter other than the original matter of a form that possesses unity of its own and that, when fully realized, achieves its own end and obeys its own laws."[2]

Hagstrum's remarks apparently apply with equal force to Lessing's concept of imitation as well. With respect to its function in the critical writings of Lessing, Harlan P. Hanson convincingly argues: "The entire essay [i.e., *Laokoon*] is obliquely directed at that system of esthetics ... to which 'imitation of nature' meant reproducing on paper its results, not its creative processes."³ Of course, Hanson does not mean to imply that creative artists are able "to imitate nature in the full sense of providing a duplicate copy of what really exists," for he readily concedes that "God has an ontological monopoly on reality" (p. 289). Even though artists are restricted to the lesser reality of their aesthetic media, Hanson nonetheless maintains that each of them "attempts, consciously or unconsciously, to conjure up in his percipient the temporary sense of another equally possible world" (p. 284). For these and similar reasons, Hanson concludes: "The creations of genius are, to Lessing, things in themselves, not things about other things" (p. 239).

It should also be stressed that the idea of imitating nature implies no slavish reproduction of the physical world. Fidelity to the external forms of nature is by no means of primary importance. Aristotle himself exonerates painters who might have erred with respect to external details by pointing out that to depict a horse throwing both right legs forward or a female deer supporting horns may be an error in medicine or some other science, but it is not necessarily a mistake in art (*Poetics*, 1460b). As Aristotle goes on to assert, the greatest offense which can be committed in the aesthetic realm consists in the failure to write or to paint imitatively. In the drafts for *Laokoon*, Lessing specifically mentions two ways, one in poetry and the other in the plastic arts, by which the mimetic intent of an artist may be frustrated. Here in reference to the enumeration of coexisting parts in poetry, Lessing underscores the inability of this technique to produce illusion by declaring: "Und wann sie [die Poesie] es thut so thut sie es nicht als nachahmende Kunst, sondern als Mittel der Erklärung." Continuing, he argues against the representation of several time periods in a single painting and similarly observes: "So wie die Mahlerey nicht nachahmende Kunst, sondern ein bloßes Mittel der Erklärung ist, wann sie verschiedne Zeiten auf einem Raume vorstellet" (XIV, 380). But these mistakes on the part of the artist result from his disregarding the spatial and temporal limitations of the medium employed, rather than from any failure to copy nature faithfully.

Perhaps the easiest way to dispose of the notion that the principle of mimesis restricts the artist to being a mere copyist of natural phenomena is to recall the fact that Aristotle held music to be the most imitative of all the arts. In an attempt to explain why Aristotle awarded this accolade to music, Katherine E. Gilbert writes: "A simple arc of stimulus and response seems to bind together the sensitive hearer and the tune. No inference is necessary. The nature of the tune is felt at once. When Aristotle declares musical modes to be the most imitative of all art forms, he means that the resemblance of music to moral states is more direct than the resemblance of a picture or statue to an emotional content... There is, as it were, an underground passage connecting the mobile energy of the soul and the mobile energy of music that gives one quick access to the other."[4] In view of the special status of music as a mimetic art, it would seem unwarranted to conclude, as many have done, that the Aristotelean concept of imitation is incompatible with the exercise of creative imagination.[5]

Despite Aristotle's attitude toward music, modern critics have for the most part considered it to be the least imitative of the arts. In mid-eighteenth-century England, moreover, its very standing as a mimetic medium came to be the subject of increasing controversy among aesthetic theorists. Even those who were willing to classify music as an imitative art seemed to feel that its efficacy needs to be explained on an entirely different basis. Undoubtedly, there was a great deal of semantic confusion among critics of that era with respect to the meaning of imitation, and many of the arguments directed against the concept of mimesis had little or nothing to do with Aristotle's formulation of the doctrine. John W. Draper sums up the situation neatly by observing: "The *Poetics* were much reverenced, but little read; and the interpretation of μίμησις depended almost altogether upon secondary sources. Some writers in fact seem to have used it without any thought of an Aristotelean origin."[6] Irrespective of the validity of the argumentation employed, the debate over the nature of mimesis resulted in music gradually being dropped from the ranks of the imitative arts during the latter half of the eighteenth century.

Generally speaking, a similar fate was to befall poetry. The initial impetus for this new view of poetry may be traced back to the publication of Edmund Burke's *Enquiry* in 1757. Here in a section entitled "POETRY not strictly an imitative art," Burke writes:

> Hence we may observe that poetry, taken in its most general sense, cannot with strict propriety be called an art of imitation. It is indeed an imitation so far as it describes the manners and passions of men which their words can express; where *animi motus effert interprete lingua.** There it is strictly imitation; and all merely *dramatic* poetry is of this sort. But *descriptive* poetry operates chiefly by *substitution*; by means of sounds, which by custom have the effect of realities. Nothing is an imitation further than it resembles some other thing; and words undoubtedly have no sort of resemblance to the ideas for which they stand.[7]

---

* By means of this citation, Burke is alluding to a passage in the *Ars Poetica* where Horace declares: "For Nature first shapes us within to meet every change of fortune... then, with the tongue for interpreter, she proclaims the emotions of the soul." See the Loeb Classical Library edition of Horace's *Satires, Epistles and Ars Poetica* (New York and London, 1926), p. 459 (ll. 108-111). The translation is by H. Rushton Fairclough.

Considering the number of unorthodox ideas set forth in the *Enquiry*, Burke's treatise was bound to evoke a mixed response from Lessing. In the letter to Mendelssohn dated February 18, 1758, he sums up his general reaction to the *Enquiry* by declaring: "Doch ,wenn schon des Verfassers Grundsätze nicht viel taugen, so ist sein Buch doch als eine Sammlung aller Eräugnungen und Wahrnehmungen, die der Philosoph bey dergleichen Untersuchungen als unstreitig annehmen muß, ungemein brauchbar. Er hat alle Materialien zu einem guten System gesammlet, die niemand besser zu brauchen wissen wird, als Sie."[8]

In many ways, Burke's idea of poetic imitation represents an attempt to carry the theory of signs through to its logical conclusion. The distinction between natural and arbitrary signs was, it should be noted, widely known in England even by those unfamiliar with the Abbé Dubos' writings owing to its use by James Harris in the second part of his *Three Treatises*. Unlike Harris, however, Burke is firmly convinced that the theory of signs requires a revaluation of poetry's status as an imitative art. If one compares Burke's criteria for imitation with the definition of natural signs, it soon becomes apparent that Burke wishes to restrict the term "imitation" to those semantic contexts in which it designates the qualities which a work of art communicates by means of "natural" signs. Although William Guild Howard makes no direct reference to the theory of signs itself, he nonetheless does much to clarify this aspect of Burke's terminology by observing: "When Burke says *imitation*, he does not mean the expression of an idea, but the copying of a model by means of symbols that have some sort of resemblance to the qualities of the model. Imitation in words is imitation *of* words, where *animi motus effert interprete lingua*. Lessing believed too firmly in Aristotle to profit by this example of Burke's independence of the Stagirite."[9]

Although the concept of mimesis is never mentioned in the letter to Nicolai dated May 26, 1769, Lessing's proposals for revising the theory of signs do much to explain the reasons why he continued to adhere to the traditional idea of poetry as an imitative art. By emphasizing the aesthetic function of such devices as meter, rhyme, metaphor, and simile, Lessing was able to demonstrate that the poet is not confined to the use of arbitrary signs. In addition to vindicating Baumgarten's view of poetry as an instrument of sensuous cognition, this emendation to the theory of signs neatly circumvents the necessity of accepting Burke's theory of imitation. Since the semiotic system utilized in the *Enquiry* presumes a rigid dichotomy between "natural" and "arbitrary" signs, it is easy to understand why Lessing saw fit to reject Burke's argument in regard to the mimetic status of descriptive poetry. If words can be transformed into natural signs through a poetic manipulation of language, there is no basis for denying descriptive poetry its place among the imitative arts. Indeed, the mimetic status of descriptive poetry is never questioned in *Laokoon* or any of its extant drafts.

Even though Lessing was never converted to the view of poetic imitation set forth in the *Enquiry*, he did not escape Burke's influence altogether. In all likelihood, it was Burke's remarks on the mimetic function of words in drama which induced Lessing to attempt a reformulation of the dramatic method in terms of the theory of signs. When Burke asserts that words in dramatic poetry are to be regarded as "strictly imitation," he is, in effect, saying that words in dramatic poetry become "natural signs of arbitrary objects."[10] But it was left to Lessing to demonstrate that words do not actually become natural signs of arbitrary objects unless they are used in a manner which is temporally congruent with the action of a play . Only in this way was it possible to clarify Aristotle's strictures against the use of narration within the context of a dramatic action. As a result of reformulating the dramatic method in terms of the theory of signs, Lessing has developed a most cogent argument on behalf of the widely-held belief that the drama is capable of achieving a greater degree of "vividness" or "illusion" than other forms of literature. It is precisely this capacity to turn words into "natural signs of arbitrary objects" that makes the dramatic method the most imitative mode of literary expression.

In addition to being an aesthetic principle,

the concept of imitation has broad philosophical implications pertaining to the essential qualities of man. According to Aristotle, the pleasure which man takes in works of imitation stems from his innate desire for the acquisition of knowledge (*Poetics*, 1448b). In the seventieth article of the *Hamburgische Dramaturgie*, Lessing restates this proposition from the philosophic perspective of the eighteenth century. As he sees it, true art is the product of an intelligence that endeavors to recreate the purposive character of nature in terms of an aesthetic medium. Although Lessing is firmly convinced that the universe forms one vast causal nexus, he also contends that only an infinite spirit is capable of perceiving the unity and purpose of nature directly. If mere mortals are ever to experience the pleasure of glimpsing the hidden harmony of the universe, they can do so only by directing their attention to limited aspects of natural phenomena, never to the whole of nature. In order to perceive the universal patterns amidst the phenomenological flux which confronts him, man must constantly exercise his powers of abstraction and elimination. The artist sets down the results of these mental operations in his works, and those who look at a painting or peruse a poem are thus spared the effort of performing this process for themselves. Art consequently calls for more than a mere realistic representation of nature. Indeed, Lessing insists that if realism were to constitute the sole criterion of artistic excellence, every dramatic monstrosity without plan or connection could then be justified by an appeal to the concept of imitation and the mimetic principle itself would lose all validity. Unless the artist imposes an aesthetic order on nature, he will, furthermore, never be capable of creating any higher type of art than the one which seeks to reproduce the colored veins of marble in plaster of Paris. In respect to the pitfalls of extreme realism, Lessing sums up his position by declaring: "Die Nachahmung der Natur müßte folglich entweder gar kein Grundsatz der Kunst seyn; oder, wenn sie es doch bliebe, würde durch ihn selbst die Kunst, Kunst zu seyn aufhören . . ." (X, 81).

At a time when the status of the *Poetics* was progressively declining among his contemporaries, Lessing chose to remain a staunch defender of the concept of imitation as well as all other aspects of Aristotle's aesthetic philosophy. While conceding that the Stagirite's arguments may occasionally stand in need of reformulation, Lessing never doubts the fundamental validity of the *Poetics*. In the concluding entry of the *Hamburgische Dramaturgie*, for example, he unequivocally asserts: "Indeß steh ich nicht an, zu bekennen, (und sollte ich in diesen erleuchteten Zeiten auch darüber ausgelacht werden!) daß ich sie für ein ebenso unfehlbares Werk halte, als die Elemente des Euklides nur immer sind" (X, 214). Although the aforementioned treatises are no longer considered infallible documents, they nevertheless remain the most important works in their respective fields. Lessing, for his part, not only succeeded in promoting a deeper appreciation of Aristotle's aesthetic theories in his own age, but is also capable of providing present-day readers with many fresh insights into the arguments of the *Poetics*.

APPENDICES

APPENDIX A: LESSING'S LETTER TO NICOLAI DATED MAY 26, 1769

Liebster Freund
. . . .
Mit der Recension meines Laokoon in dem letzten Stücke Ihrer Bibliothek, kann ich sehr wohl zufrieden seyn. Ich denke, daß ich den Namen des Recensenten schon weiß. Aber was gehen mich Namen an? Die Person werde ich doch nicht kennen lernen. Wenn er die Fortsetzung meines Buches wird gelesen haben, soll er wohl finden, daß mich seine Einwürfe nicht treffen. Ich räume ihm ein, daß Verschiedenes darin nicht bestimmt genug ist: aber wie kann es, da ich nur kaum den Einen Unterschied zwischen der Poesie und Malerey zu betrachten angefangen habe, welcher aus dem Gebrauche ihrer Zeichen entspringt, in so fern die einen in der Zeit, und die andern im Raume existiren? Beyde können eben sowohl natürlich, als willkührlich seyn; folglich muß es nothwendig eine doppelte Malerey und eine doppelte Poesie geben: wenigstens von den beyden eine höhere und eine niedrige Gattung. Die Malerey braucht entweder coexistirende Zeichen, welche natürlich sind, oder welche willkührlich sind; und eben diese Verschiedenheit findet sich auch bey den consecutiven Zeichen der Poesie. Denn es ist eben so wenig wahr, daß die Malerey sich nur natürlicher Zeichen bediene, als es wahr ist, daß die Poesie nur willkührliche Zeichen brauche. Aber das ist gewiß, daß je mehr sich die Malerey von den natürlichen Zeichen entfernt, oder die natürlichen mit willkührlichen vermischt, desto mehr entfernt sie sich von ihrer Vollkommenheit: wie hingegen

die Poesie sich um so mehr ihrer Vollkommenheit nähert, je mehr sie ihre willkührlichen Zeichen den natürlichen näher bringt. Folglich ist die höhere Malerey die, welche nichts als natürliche Zeichen im Raume brauchet, und die höhere Poesie die, welche nichts als natürliche Zeichen in der Zeit brauchet. Folglich kann auch weder die historische noch die allegorische Malerey zur höhern Malerey gehören, als welche nur durch die dazu kommenden willkührlichen Zeichen verständlich werden können. Ich nenne aber willkührliche Zeichen in der Malerey nicht allein alles, was zum Costume gehört, sondern auch einen großen Theil des Körperlichen Ausdrucks selbst. Zwar sind diese Dinge eigentlich nicht in der Malerey willkührlich; ihre Zeichen sind in der Malerey auch natürliche Zeichen: aber es sind doch *natürliche* Zeichen von *willkührlichen* Dingen, welche unmöglich eben das allgemeine Verständniß, eben die geschwinde und schnelle Wirkung haben können, als *natürliche* Zeichen von *natürlichen* Dingen. Wenn aber bey diesen Schönheit das höchste Gesetz ist, und mein Recensent selbst zugiebt (S. 353), daß der Maler alsdann auch in der That am meisten Maler sey: so sind wir ja einig, und, wie gesagt, sein Einwurf trifft mich nicht. Denn alles was ich noch von der Malerey gesagt habe, betrifft nur die Malerey nach ihrer höchsten und eigenthümlichsten Wirkung. Ich habe nie geläugnet, daß sie auch, außer dieser, noch Wirkungen genug haben könne; ich habe nur läugnen wollen, daß ihr alsdann der Name Malerey weniger

APPENDIX A

zukomme. Ich habe nie an den Wirkungen der historischen und allegorischen Malerey gezweifelt, noch weniger habe ich diese Gattungen aus der Welt verbannen wollen; ich habe nur gesagt, daß in diesen der Maler weniger Maler ist, als in Stücken wo die Schönheit seine einzige Absicht ist. Und giebt mir das der Recensent zu? - Nun noch ein Wort von der Poesie, damit Sie nicht mißverstehen, was ich eben gesagt habe. Die Poesie muß schlechterdings ihre willkührlichen Zeichen zu natürlichen zu erheben suchen; und nur dadurch unterscheidet sie sich von der Prose, und wird Poesie. Die Mittel, wodurch sie dieses thut, sind der Ton, die Worte, die Stellung der Worte, das Sylbenmaß, Figuren und Tropen, Gleichnisse u.s.w. Alle diese Dinge bringen die willkührlichen Zeichen den natürlichen näher; aber sie machen sie nicht zu natürlichen Zeichen: folglich sind alle Gattungen, die sich nur dieser Mittel bedienen, als die niedern Gattungen der Poesie zu betrachten; und die höchste Gattung der Poesie ist die, welche die willkührlichen Zeichen gänzlich zu natürlichen Zeichen macht. Das ist aber die dramatische; denn in dieser hören die Worte auf willkührliche Zeichen zu seyn, und werden *natürliche* Zeichen willkührlicher Dinge. Daß die dramatische Poesie die höchste, ja die einzige Poesie ist, hat schon Aristoteles gesagt, und er giebt der Epopee nur in so fern die zweyte Stelle, als sie größten Theils dramatisch ist, oder seyn kann. Der Grund, den er davon angiebt, ist zwar nicht der meinige; aber er läßt sich auf meinen reduciren, und wird

APPENDIX A

nur durch diese Reduction auf meinen, vor aller falschen Anwendung gesichert.

Wenn Sie mit Hrn. Moses eine halbe Stunde darüber plaudern wollen, so melden Sie mir doch, was er dazu sagt. Die weitere Ausführung davon soll den dritten Theil meines Laokoons ausmachen.

. . . .

Dero ergebenster Freund,
Lessing

Cited from L-M, XVII, 289-292.

APPENDIX B: ARISTOTLE'S ARGUMENTS ON THE SUPERIORITY OF THE DRAMA

The question may be raised which is superior, the epic or the tragic form of imitation. For if the less vulgar art is superior, and the one which is addressed to a better class of spectators is of that description, it would be clear that the one which imitates anything and everything is vulgar. For it is because they assume that the public will not 'get it' unless (the actor) himself exaggerates that they indulge in a plethora of movement, like the bad flute-players who writhe when they have to represent a discus-throw, or pull and haul at the chorus-leader when they are rendering the *Scylla*. So (they say) tragedy is like that, the way the earlier actors used to consider the later ones: Mynniscus, for example, used to call Callippides "ape," on the ground that he exaggerated too much, and a similar opinion used to be current about Pindarus too. As the latter stand in relation to them (the older actors), then, so the whole art stands in relation to the epic. So people maintain that the latter is addressed to a cultivated audience, <who> have no need of the dance-figures, while the tragic art is addressed to a low and worthless one. If then it is vulgar, it must obviously be inferior.

In the first place the accusation is not against the art of poetry but against that of acting; because it is possible to exaggerate with one's gestures in epic recitation also, which is what Sosistratus used to do, or in lyric competition, as Mnasitheus of Opus used to do. Secondly, not all dramatic movement is to be censored out either, if not all dancing is, but only that of low characters, which is what Callippides was criticized for and others are nowadays: for imitating low women, as they say. Further, tragedy, does its work even without movement (performance), like the epic; for it can convey its qualities through reading. If, then, it is superior in its other aspects, this reproach does not necessarily attach to it.

Then further, because it has everything the epic has (it can even use its verse), and no small element besides: the music [and the effects of spectacle], through which the spectator's enjoyment is most vividly aroused; and then it also has the element of vividness, in reading as well as in performance. Again, by virtue of the fact that the end of the imitation comes in a shorter span. For a thing is more enjoyable in concentrated form than when diluted by a great deal of time: I mean for example if someone should put the *Oedipus* of Sophocles in as many verses as the *Iliad* (has). Still less (enjoyable) is the (kind of) unified imitation produced by the epic poets, [A sign ... are made] so that when they do compose a single plot, either it is presented in brief form and gives the impression of being curtailed or it follows the length of the norm and strikes us as heavily diluted. (<A sign of this: from any (epic) imitation, no matter what its qualities, a number of tragedies are made: > I mean if it is composed of a number of actions; for example the *Iliad* has a number of parts of that kind [and the *Odyssey*], which have bulk in

APPENDIX B

themselves too – and it [and some such poems] is as well constructed as the epic permits, i.e., is, as much as it can be, an imitation of a single action.)

Cited from Gerald F. Else's *Aristotle's Poetics: The Argument* (Cambridge, Mass., 1957), pp. 633-634, 639. On p. xvi of the introduction, Else explains the function of the sigla in his translation as follows:

[ ] An interpolation, not by Aristotle.

< > A word or words not preserved in our Greek MSS, but presumed here to have been in Aristotle's autograph.

( ) Around one or two words, indicates an explanation or amplification of a term by the translator; otherwise, a parenthesis by Aristotle himself.

APPENDIX C: MENDELSSOHN'S "VON DER ILLUSION"

§ 11.

Wenn eine Nachahmung so viel Ähnliches mit dem Urbilde hat, daß sich unsere Sinne wenigstens einen Augenblick bereden können, das Urbild selbst zu sehen, so nenne ich diesen Betrug eine ästhetische Illusion.

Der Dichter muß vollkommen sinnlich reden; daher müssen uns alle seine Reden ästhetisch illudiren.

§ 12.

Soll eine Nachahmung schön seyn, so muß sie uns ästhetisch illudiren; die obern Seelenkräfte aber müssen überzeugt seyn, daß es eine Nachahmung, und nicht die Natur selbst sei.

Denn das Vergnügen, das uns die Nachahmung gewährt, besteht in der anschauenden Erkenntniß der Übereinstimmung derselben mit dem Urbilde. Es gehören also folgende beide Urtheile dazu, wenn wir an einer Nachahmung Vergnügen finden wollen: "dieses Bild gleicht dem Urbilde;" – "dieses Bild ist nicht das Urbild selbst." – Man sieht leicht, daß jenes Urtheil vorangehen muß; daher muß die Überzeugung von der Ähnlichkeit intuitive, oder vermittelst der Illusion; die Überzeugung hingegen, daß es nicht das Urbild selbst sei, kann etwas später erfolgen, und daher mehr von der symbolischen abhangen.

§ 13.

Da uns die Nachahmung an und für sich selbst nicht so sehr vergnügt, als die Geschicklichkeit des Künstlers, der sie zu treffen gewußt hat, so setzen wir uns bei der Beurtheilung der schönen Künste über alles hinweg, wozu keine größere Geschicklichkeit von Seiten des Künstlers erfordert worden wäre, es nachzuahmen.

a) Daher sind die äußerlichen Verzierungen bei einer dramatischen Vorstellung nur zufällig, und öfters schädlich, wenn sie durch ihre eigene Schönheit unsere Aufmerksamkeit von der Vorstellung abwenden. Es ist genug, wenn die Verzierungen nicht durch einen offenbaren Widerspruch der Illusion schaden.

b) Ja es ist nicht einmal nöthig, daß ein dramatisches Stück aufgeführt würde, um zu gefallen. Wer beim Lesen urtheilen kann, ob der Dichter sein Stück mit der gehörigen Kunst ausgearbeitet, und ob er es so gemacht hat, daß es durch die lebendige Vorstellung eines höheren Grades der Nachahmung fähig werden kann; der kann die äußere Vorstellung leicht entbehren.

§ 14.

Das beste Mittel, uns intuitive von dem Werthe der Nachahmung zu überzeugen, ist, wenn vermittelst der Illusion unangenehme Leidenschaften in uns erregt werden.

a) Wenn wir eine gemalte Schlange plötzlich

anblicken, so gefällt sie uns desto besser, je mehr wir uns davor erschreckt haben. Aristoteles glaubt, wir ergötzten uns, weil wir von der vermeinten Gefahr befreit worden wären. Allein wie unnatürlich ist diese Erklärung. Ich glaube vielmehr, der kurze Schrecken überführt uns intuitive, daß das Urbild getroffen sei.

b) Daher gefallen uns alle unangenehme Affekten in der Nachahmung. Der Musikus kann uns zornig, betrübt, verzweiflungsvoll u.s.w. machen, und wir wissen ihm Dank für die unangenehmen Leidenschaften, die er in uns erregt hat. Man sieht aber, daß in diesen Fällen das zweite Urtheil: diese Affecten sind nur nachgeahmt, unmittelbar auf den Affect folgen muß; weil sonst die unangenehme Empfindung, die aus dem Affecte entspringt, größer seyn würde, als die angenehme, die eine Wirkung der Nachahmung ist.

c) Aus diesen Gründen lassen sich die Gränzen des bekannten Gesetzes bestimmen: *die schönen Künste sind eine Nachahmung der Natur, aber nicht die Natur selbst.*

Cited from *Lessings Briefwechsel mit Mendelssohn und Nicolai über das Trauerspiel, nebst verwandten Schriften Nicolais und Mendelssohns,* ed. Robert Petsch (Leipzig, 1910), pp. 134-135.

NOTES

NOTES I: LESSING'S ARGUMENT TO NICOLAI

[1] *Lessings sämtliche Schriften*, 3rd ed., ed. Karl Lachmann and Franz Muncker (Stuttgart and Leipzig, 1886-1924), XVII, 287 – hereafter cited as L-M in the notes. All parenthetic numerals following quotations from Lessing within the text refer respectively to the volume and page number of this edition.

[2] Although René Wellek has recently offered an explication of this letter, his interpretation is completely incompatible with the analysis presented here. See *A History of Modern Criticism: 1750-1950*, I (New Haven, Conn., 1955), 164-165.

[3] Lessing's high regard for Dubos' treatise may be discerned from the fact that he went as far as to translate the last third of the *Réflexions* for his periodical *Theatralische Bibliothek* in 1755. Lessing's translation bears the title heading "Des Abts du Bos Ausschweifung von den theatralischen Vorstellungen der Alten" and is accompanied by a preface in which he provides a brief summary of the first two parts. His familiarity with the contents of Dubos' work may therefore be presumed. See L-M, VI, 247-248 for a reprint of Lessing's preface.

[4] Moses Mendelssohn, *Schriften zur Philosophie, Aesthetik und Apologetik*, ed. Moritz Brasch (Leipzig, 1880), II, 153. Since Mendelssohn cites the articulated sounds of all languages, the letters of the alphabet, and the hieroglyphic signs of the ancients as examples of arbitrary signs, it would appear that the entire realm of poetry falls within the scope of the aesthetic philosophy advanced in *Laokoon*. There is, however, at least one major exception – namely, poetry written in Chinese ideograms. In a study completed shortly before his death in 1908 entitled *Chinese Written Character as a Medium for Poetry* (New York, n.d.), Ernest Fenellosa considers the Chinese sentence "Man Sees Horse" and observes: "Chinese notation is something much more than arbitrary symbols. It is based upon a vivid shorthand picture of the operations of nature. In

the algebraic figure and in the spoken word there is no natural connection between thing and sign: all depends upon sheer convention. But the Chinese method follows natural suggestion. First stands the man on his two legs. Second, his eye moves through space: a bold figure represented by running legs under an eye, a modified picture of an eye, a modified picture of running legs, but unforgettable once you have seen it. Third stands the horse on his four legs ... The group holds something of the quality of a continuous moving picture" (p. 58). Because Chinese ideograms are not entirely arbitrary and exhibit aspects of natural signs, poetry written in Chinese characters forms a special category to which the basic premise of *Laokoon* in regard to the conventional nature of human discourse does not wholly apply.

[5] On pp. 79-88 of his book *Lessing's Laokoon* (Lancaster, Pa., 1940), Fred O. Nolte attempts a general assessment of the theory of signs. Since Nolte invests the terms "natural" and "arbitrary" with semantic associations extraneous to Dubos' theory, his appraisal does not merit serious consideration. His discussion, moreover, is based on the drafts for *Laokoon* and contains no reference to the letter of May 26, 1769.

[6] Garve's review has been reprinted by Hugo Blümner in the appendix to his critical edition of *Laokoon*. See *Lessings Laokoon*, 2nd ed. (Berlin, 1880), pp. 683-703.

[7] L-M, XVII, 290-291. The italics in the letter intermittently quoted on pp. 5-9 are those of Lessing; all italicization in future citations will be restricted solely to that found in the original source. The full text of Lessing's argument to Nicolai is reproduced in Appendix A on pp. 93-96.

NOTES II: THE AESTHETIC THEORIES OF THE ABBÉ DUBOS

[1] *Réflexions critique sur la poésie et sur la peinture*, quatrième édition revûe, corrigée & augmentée par l'Auteur (Paris, 1740), II, 325-326 (sec. XXII).

[2] See especially the preface to Félibien's *Conférences de l'Academie Royale de Peinture et de Sculpture* (Paris, 1669). Here Félibien puts the still-life and lanscape painter at the bottom of a hierarchical classification of artists. A strikingly similar typological ranking of painters may be found in Lessing's preliminary drafts for *Laokoon*. See L-M, XIV, 415. Lessing's indebtedness to Félibien in this context is discussed on pp. 20-21 of Rensselaer W. Lee's essay entitled *Ut pictura poesis: The Humanistic Theory of Painting* (New York, 1967). Lee's essay was originally published in *The Art Bulletin*, XXII (December 1940), 199-269.

[3] See the unpubl. diss. (Harvard, 1959), "Leibniz and Lessing's Critical Thought," p. 215. Cf. E. H. Gombrich's assertion: "The more one reads the Laocoon, the stronger becomes the impression that it is not so much a book about as against the visual arts: 'If Painting is really Poetry's sister', Lessing remarks in it, 'let her at least not be a jealous sister'" ("Lessing," *The Proceedings of the British Academy*, XLIII [1957], 140). The passage from *Laokoon* cited by Gombrich may be found in Ch. viii (L-M, IX, 65).

NOTES III: LESSING'S CONCEPT OF POETRY

[1] Langer, *Philosophy in a New Key*, 3rd. ed. (Cambridge, Mass., 1957), p. 93.

[2] Cf. Goethe's words to J. D. Falk on June 14, 1809: "Wir sprechen überhaupt viel zu viel. Wir sollten weniger sprechen und mehr zeichnen. Ich meinerseits möchte mir das Reden ganz abgewöhnen und wie die bildende Natur in lauter Zeichnungen fortsprechen... Je mehr ich darüber nachdenke, es ist etwas so Unnützes, so Müßiges, ich möchte fast sagen Geckenhaftes im Reden..." See *Gespräche*, ed. F. and W. von Biedermann (Leipzig, 1909), II, 40 (no. 1185).

[3] The designation *Weltweisheit* came into general use owing to Wolff's practice of employing this term in place of the word *Philosophie* in his German writings. The term was, it should be noted, previously used by Christian Thomasius for the purpose of distinguishing between theology (*Gottesgelahrtheit*) and the more secular forms of philosophic activity. Wolff, however, abandons the limitation to the finite imposed by Thomasius and adopts *Weltweisheit* as a more colloquial substitute for the word "philosophy." See Johann Eduard Erdmann, *Grundriß der Geschichte der Philosophie*, 4th ed. (Berlin, 1896), II, 195, 200.

[4] In the introduction to their translation of Baumgarten's *Meditationes philosophicae de nonnullis ad poema pertinentibus*, Karl Aschenbrenner and William B. Holther state: "Whatever may be said for or against Baumgarten's bias toward a cognitive theory of art, it is at any rate time to challenge the leading artistic dogma of the past two centuries, that art is and of right ought to be solely or preëminently the expression of emotion. We have arrived at the place where such a dogma is no longer obvious as a description nor wise if it is taken as advice" (*Baumgarten's Reflections on Poetry* [Berkeley and Los Angeles, 1954], pp. 8-9). However, nowhere in the introduction do Aschenbrenner and Holther make reference to the work of any twentieth-century philosophers who have endeavor-

ed to reformulate aesthetic theory on a non-emotive basis.

[5] Leibniz, *Philosophical Papers and Letters*, trans. and ed. Leroy E. Loemker (Chicago, 1956), I, 448. In proposition twelve of the *Meditationes*, Baumgarten notes that it is possible for the same object of perception to evoke a clear idea in one individual and an obscure idea in another. Immanuel Kant, himself a proponent of *Weltweisheit* until the late seventeen-sixties, attempts to clarify this paradox in section five of his introduction to the compendium on logic which was published under the supervision of his pupil Gottlob Benjamin Jäsche. Here Kant writes: "Sieht z.B. ein Wilder ein Haus aus der Ferne, dessen Gebrauch er nicht kennt: so hat er zwar eben dasselbe Objekt, wie ein anderer, der es bestimmt als eine für Menschen eingerichtete Wohnung kennt, in der Vorstellung vor sich. Aber der Form nach ist dieses Erkenntnis eines und desselben Objekts in beiden verschieden... Die Verschiedenheit der Form des Erkenntnisses beruht auf einer Bedingung, die alles Erkennen begleitet – auf dem *Bewußtsein*. Bin ich mir der Vorstellung bewußt: so ist sie *klar*; bin ich mir derselben nicht bewußt, *dunkel*." See *Werke*, ed. Wilhelm Weischedel (Frankfurt, 1956-1964), III, 457.

[6] Although the criteria of clearness and distinctness also play a prominent role in the writings of Descartes, the meaning which the French philosopher assigns to these terms does not fully conform to the definitions from Leibniz discussed below. See Principles XLV and XLVI in the First Part of *Principia philosophicae* (1644) for Descartes' most explicit analysis of these criteria.

[7] *Philosophical Papers and Letters*, I, 449. In his article "Herder and the *Aufklärung*: A Leibnizian Context," Israel S. Stamm demonstrates the operation of confused cognition as follows: "The color red, as I normally experience it, is a confused idea, 'confused' being used here, it should well be noted, in a more original

etymological sense of 'con-fusus,' fused together into a whole. A confused idea is simply a whole, unanalyzed idea. Through the senses I normally experience whole, confused ideas: the color red, that chair, that man. But if I were to analyze the color red scientifically, or the idea of man to arrive at a definition of him, I should be moving to distinct ideas." See *Germanic Review*, XXXVIII (May 1963), 198 (n. 2).

[8] Among the more prominent practitioners of *Weltweisheit*, Johann Georg Sulzer rejects the bifurcation of the cognitive faculties described above in favor of a tripartite division. See Armand Nivelle's *Les théories esthétiques en Allemagne de Baumgarten à Kant* (Paris, 1955), p. 86.

[9] Schmidt, *Lessing*, 4th ed. (Berlin, 1923), I, 252.

[10] In proposition three of *Meditationes*, for example, Baumgarten demonstrates their fundamental identity as follows: "By *sensate representations* we mean representations received through the lower part of the cognitive faculty ... since, on the other hand, a confused representation, along with an obscure one, is received through the lower part of the cognitive faculty, we can apply the same name to confused representations, in order that they may be distinguished from concepts distinct at all possible levels." See p. 38 of the previously-cited translation by Aschenbrenner and Holther. Kant, however, explicitly rejects the semantic equivalence of the words *verworren* and *sinnlich* as postulated by the *Weltweisen* and draws a distinction between these two terms, among other places, in article seven of his treatise entitled *De mundi sensibilis* (1791) and in section five of his introduction to *Logik* (1800).

[11] In proposition ninety-one of *Psychologia rationalis* (1734), Wolff states: "Die sinnlichen Ideen sind ähnlich dem Objekt, welches sie darstellen..." See p. 5 of Julius Baumann's *Wolffsche Begriffsbestimmungen* (Leipzig, 1910).

[12] Translators of *Laokoon* often fail to differentiate between these two words and treat them as synonyms – at times rendering the term *deutlich* as "clear" and *klar* as "distinct." Of course, such errors are precluded when these lexical items are used in tandem in the stock phrase *klar und deutlich* (see previous citation from Ch. xvii of *Laokoon* on p. 21).

[13] Robert Graves, trans. *The Anger of Achilles: Homer's Iliad* (Garden City, N.Y., 1959), p. 66 (Bk. II, ll. 478-484).

[14] L-M, XIV, 337. This passage as well as several others previously cited from *Laokoon* and its drafts should suffice to invalidate the views recently expressed by Klaus R. Scherpe on p. 114 of his *Gattungspoetik im 18. Jahrhundert* (Stuttgart, 1968). With respect to Lessing's activities in the field of literary criticism, Scherpe maintains: "Baumgartens Erkenntnislehre des 'Sinnlichen' lag außerhalb seines Blickfeldes, da sie die praktischen Forderungen der Kritik, die der Kunstrichter zu erfüllen suchte, unberücksichtig ließ." In a footnote referring to the preceding statement, Scherpe further remarks: "Lediglich in der gemeinsam mit Mendelssohn verfaßten Schrift 'Pope ein Metaphysiker!' (1755) kommt Baumgartens Definition der Poesie zur Geltung. Dieser Passus ist aber wohl als Mendelssohns Anteil anzusehen." Of course, my own findings regarding the extent of Lessing's reliance on Baumgarten's aesthetic theories run diametrically counter to Scherpe's assessment of the situation.

[15] Baumgarten himself expected to include a semiotic system in the projected third and concluding part of his *Aesthetica*, but failed to live long enough to fulfill this intention. Although Baumgarten's pupil Georg Friedrich Meier did make an attempt to develop a general theory of aesthetic signs in the treatise entitled *Anfangsgründe aller Schönen Wissenschaften* (Halle, 1748-1750), Sigmund von Lempicki dismisses Meier's effort as totally inadequate and declares: "Den

eigentlichen Anstoß für die Verwertung der Zeichentheorie zur näheren Bestimmung ästhetischer Gegenstände gab J. Harris in seinen 'Three Treatises.'" Lempicki also goes on to emphasize the special importance of James Harris's *Three Treatises* (London, 1744) in regard to stimulating the composition of *Laokoon* and asserts: "Von Harris ist auch Mendelssohn angeregt worden, ohne den, nach Erich Schmidts Bemerkung, vielleicht der Laokoon nicht zustande gekommen wäre ... Mendelssohns Anregungen folgend und die Ideen von Harris verwertend, gelangte abei erst Lessing zu einer klaren Scheidung der Gebiete der Poesie und der Malerei." See *Geschichte der deutschen Literaturwissenschaft bis zum Ende des 18. Jahrhunderts*, 2. vermehrte Auflage (Göttingen, 1968), pp. 311-312. However, Harris's terminology clearly indicates that the semiotic system which he advances in the second of the three treatises was itself derived from the Abbé Dubos' theory of *signes naturels* and *signes artificiels*. In the first chapter of the second treatise, for example, Harris defines the areas of similarity and difference between music, painting, and poetry as follows: "They *agree*, by being *all* Mimetic or Imitative. They *differ*, as they imitate by *different Media*; Painting, by *Figure* and *Colour*; Music, by *Sound* and *Motion*; Painting and Music, by *Media which are Natural*; Poetry, for the greater Part, by *a Medium, which is Artificial*" (p. 58). Unlike Lessing, however, Harris never questions Dubos' assumption that words in poetry (except for instances of onomatopoetic usage) are fated to remain immutably "arbitrary" in character.

[16] There are, of course, few contemporary aestheticians who formally sanction the theory of signs. In the work entitled *Art and Illusion* (New York, 1960), E. H. Gombrich sums up the theoretical objections to the concept of natural signs as follows: "Everything points to the conclusion that the phrase the 'language of art' is more than a loose metaphor, that even to describe

the visible world in images we need a developed system of schemata. This conclusion rather clashes with the traditional distinction, often discussed in the eighteenth century, between spoken words which are conventional signs and painting which uses 'natural' signs to 'imitate' reality. It is a plausible distinction, but it has led to certain difficulties. If we assume, with this tradition, that natural signs can simply be copied from nature, the history of art represents a complete puzzle. It has become increasingly clear since the late ninteenth century that primitive art and child art use a language of symbols rather than 'natural signs.' To account for this fact it was postulated that there must be a special kind of art grounded not on seeing but rather on knowledge, an art which operates with 'conceptual images.' The child – it is argued – does not look at trees; he is satisfied with the 'conceptual' schema of a tree that fails to correspond to any reality since it does not embody the characteristics of say, birch or beech, let alone those of individual trees. This reliance on construction rather than on imitation was attributed to the peculiar mentality of children and primitives who live in a world of their own" (p. 87). Mendelssohn's definition of natural signs, however, is broad enough in scope to include the representations of both primitive art and child art. If one recalls that Lessing designates "form" and "color" as the signs employed by the plastic artist, it is clear that all art (with the sole exception of non-objective art) communicates through natural signs. All that is necessary for "form" and "color" to function as natural signs is for the artist to use them in a representational context. The degree of realism or abstraction is in no way a decisive factor.

NOTES IV. ARISTOTLE AND THE NECESSITY FOR THEATRICAL PERFORMANCE

[1] Szarota, *Lessings "Laokoon"* (Weimar, 1959), p. 165.
[2] Gottschlich, *Lessing's aristotelische Studien* (Berlin, 1876), pp. 126-127. Since Wellek makes no mention of Gottschlich's work in his bibliography, it may be assumed that he arrived at his solution independently.
[3] *Poetics*, 1462a, 14-16. The above citation is taken from Gerald F. Else's translation and commentary entitled *Aristotle's Poetics: The Argument* (Cambridge, Mass., 1957). Unless otherwise indicated, all subsequent quotations from the *Poetics* are to be attributed to this source.
[4] L-M, XIV, 430-431. See also Dubos, *Réflexions*, I, 438 (sec. XLV).
[5] Emphasizing the extent to which Lessing anticipated Wagner, Jack M. Stein remarks: "Indeed, [Wagner's] *The Art Work of the Future* is in some ways the answer to the tentative suggestions toward a synthesis made by Lessing in the sketches for a Part II of *Laocoön*." See p. 63 of *Richard Wagner and the Synthesis of the Arts* (Detroit, 1960).
[6] Plato, *Laws*, Bk. II, 658c-658d.
[7] See p. 35 in the present chapter.
[8] Else, p. 641. Else's abstract is derived from section 1462a-b, the text of which is fully reproduced in Appendix B. The notation employed in Else's abstract represents the standard subdivision of page 1462 from the edition of Aristotle's works prepared for the Berlin Academy by Immanuel Beker in 1830. The letters *a* and *b* signify the left- and right-hand columns respectively, and the numerals refer to the individual lines in each column. In the previous quotation from Gottschlich's *Lessing's aristotelische Studien*, the fourth item in Else's tabulation was designated as Aristotle's *second* argument.
[9] In Else's more recent translation of the *Poetics*, which is based on the 1965 Oxford Classical Text edition prepared by Rudolf Kassel, the wording of the above passage has been revised so that it now reads: "If then,

NOTES IV

tragedy is superior on all these counts and also with respect to its function as an art (for the two arts should produce not any random pleasure but the one we have specified), it is evident that it must be superior, since it attains the purpose better than the epic does." See Aristotle's *Poetics* (Ann Arbor, 1967), p. 75.

[10] *Poetics*, 1453b. See pp. 48-49 for a complete citation of the opening section of chapter fourteen.

[11] See p. 642 of Else's commentary for an explanation concerning the equivalency of the terms "movement" and "performance" in this context.

[12] Else, pp. 643-644. Cf. R. P. Blackmur, *Language as Gesture: Essays in Poetry* (New York, 1952), pp. 12-13. Here Blackmur proposes that one of the main tasks of a writer consists in finding ways in which "the physical gesture with face and hands and vocal gesture in shifting inflections" may be incorporated into the written language. Pursuing this line of thought Blackmur further stipulates: "And he [the writer] must do this by making his written words sound in the inward ear of his reader, and so play upon each other by concert and opposition and pattern that they not only drag after them the gestures of life but produce a new gesture of their own."

[13] L-M, IV, 53-54. Here, for example, Lessing writes: "Wer weis nicht, daß die dramatische Poesie nur durch die Vorstellung in dasjenige Licht gesetzt werde, worinne ihre wahre Schönheit am deutlichsten in die Augen fällt? Sie reizet, wenn man sie lieset, allein sie reizet ungleich mehr, wenn man sie hört und sieht ... Wer sieht also nicht, daß die Vorstellung ein nothwendiges Theil der dramatischen Poesie sey?"

[14] The above account concerning Lessing's early acquaintance with the *Poetics* is based on pp. 2-4 in the previously-cited study by Gottschlich.

[15] *Poetics*, 1450b, 17-20. Listed in order of relative importance, the six constituent parts form the following sequence: plot, character, thought, speech, song, and

visual appearance. By the term "visual appearance" (ὄψις), Aristotle is most probably referring to the masks and costumes of the actors, rather than to the total effect of the staging. See Else, pp. 233-234.

[16] *Poetics*, 1453b, 1-4. This section of the *Poetics* also figures prominently in the eightieth article of the *Hamburgische Dramaturgie*, where Lessing takes issue with Voltaire's contention that the small physical dimensions of the French stage together with its poor scenery combine to make it difficult for the poet to achieve a truly tragic effect. "Sollte es möglich seyn," he asks rhetorically, "daß der Mangel eines geräumlichen Theaters und guter Verzierungen, einen solchen Einfluß auf das Genie der Dichter gehabt hätte? Ist es wahr, daß jede tragische Handlung Pomp und Zurüstungen erfordert? Oder sollte der Dichter nicht vielmehr sein Stück so einrichten, daß es auch ohne diese Dinge seine völlige Wirkung hervorbrächte?" (X, 125). By way of rebuttal, Lessing deems it sufficient to refer his readers to the first half of the passage from the *Poetics* cited above. To judge solely by the context in which Lessing invokes Aristotle's authority on this occasion, it is not quite clear how he interprets the intent of these lines from the *Poetics*. For the sake of remaining consistent with the position previously established in article seventy-seven, however, Lessing would be compelled to reject any interpretation of this passage which holds that Aristotle believed it possible for an outline of the plot of a play to do the emotional work of tragedy. Since article seventy-seven states that pity and fear can only be induced by means of the dramatic method, Lessing would be obliged to contend that the author of the *Poetics* had a reading of the full text of the play in mind. While most commentators (including Else himself) are inclined toward the former interpretation, a few prominent scholars have come out in favor of the latter view. In his own commentary to the *Poetics*, Else lists

S. H. Butcher, Alfred Gudemann, and E. Valgimigli among those who believe that Aristotle has a reading of the whole play in mind. Specifically, Else calls his readers' attention to p. 261 in Butcher's *Aristotle's Theory of Poetry*, 4th ed. (London, 1932) and to p. 252 in Gudemann's *Aristoteles Über die Dichtkunst* (Berlin, 1934). However, no page reference is given for Valgimigli's *Aristotele Poetica*, 2nd ed. (Bari, 1934). See Else, p. 408 (n. 3).

[17] My conclusion in regard to this aspect of Lessing's dramatic theory is in no way contradicted by the opening section of article eighty in the *Hamburgische Dramaturgie*. Here the author maintains that the evocation of pity and fear ought rightly to be the prime objective of any serious dramatist and begins his argument by posing the following rhetorical question: "Wozu die sauere Arbeit der dramatische Form? wozu ein Theater erbauet, Männer und Weiber verkleidet, Gedächtnisse gemartert, die ganze Stadt auf einen Platz geladen? wenn ich mit meinem Werke, und mit der Aufführung desselben, weiter nichts hervorbringen will, als einige von den Regungen, die eine gute Erzehlung, von jedem zu Hause in seinem Winkel gelesen, ungefehr auch hervorbringen würde" (L-M, X, 123). It should, however, be emphasized that Lessing's remark concerning "eine gute Erzehlung" pertains only to the reading of *narrative* works and was not intended to refer to the reading of *dramatic* texts. See Lessing's comments on Gerstenberg's *Ugolino* cited below on pp. 64-65 of Ch. vi.

NOTES V. THE NATURE OF ILLUSION

[1] Perhaps the most extensive account of Lessing's and Mendelssohn's views on the subject of illusion is set forth on pp. 12-54 of Ursula Liebrecht Jarvis's unpubl. diss. (Columbia, 1961), "Theories of Illusion and Distance in Drama: From Lessing to Brecht." My own analysis of Lessing's position, however, differs in several significant respects from her treatment of the topic.

[2] Robertson, *Lessing's Dramatic Theory* (Cambridge, 1939), pp. 430-431.

[3] In addition to the ideas expressed in the 1756-57 correspondence with Lessing and Nicolai, Mendelssohn also discusses the concept of illusion in the following works: (1) *Briefe über die Empfindungen* (1755); (2) *Von der Herrschaft über die Neigungen* (written in 1757, but not published until 1831); (3) *Von den Quellen und Verbindungen der schönen Künste* (published in 1757, later revised in 1761 and republished under the title *Ueber die Hauptgrundsätze der schönen Künste*); and (4) *Rhapsodie, oder Zusätze zu den Briefen über die Empfindungen* (1761, later revised in 1771).

[4] The term is still commonly used in this sense today. In the glossary to Mordecai Gorelik's *New Theatres for Old* (New York, 1940), for example, the goal of illusion is described as follows: "It attempts to persuade an audience that the actions on stage have not been planned by theatre workers but are actually taking place in the natural world. It tries to make the audience feel that they are not in a theatre but have been transported to the scene of the events in the natural world" (pp. 483-484).

[5] In citing the passage on illusion from Lessing's letter to Mendelssohn dated December 18, 1756, Robertson calls attention to the similarity between the views expressed on that occasion and those to be found in the chapter from the *Réflexions* entitled "Que le plaisir que nous avons au Théâtre n'est point produit par l'illusion." See *Lessing's Dramatic Theory*, p. 430

(n. 1). It should be easier to appreciate the extent of Dubos' influence on Lessing during this period if one recalls that he saw fit to translate the last third of the *Réflexions* for his *Theatralische Bibliothek* only a short time before in 1755.

[6] *Lessings Briefwechsel mit Mendelssohn und Nicolai über das Trauerspiel, nebst verwandten Schriften Nicolais und Mendelssohns*, ed. Robert Petsch (Leipzig, 1910), p. 134. See Appendix C for the complete text of "Von der Illusion."

[7] In the letter to Nicolai dated April 2, 1757, Lessing raises further objections to the theory of aesthetic illusion and discounts the need for a complete deception of the senses by arguing: "Ist die Nachahmung nur dann erst zu ihrer Vollkommenheit gelangt, wenn man sie für die Sache selbst zu nehmen verleitet wird; so kann z.E. von den nachgeahmten Leidenschaften nichts wahr seyn, was nicht auch von den wirklichen Leidenschaften gilt. Das Vergnügen über die Nachahmung, als Nachahmung, ist eigentlich das Vergnügen über die Geschicklichkeit des Künstlers, welches nicht anders, als aus angestellten Vergleichungen, entstehen kann; es ist daher weit später, als das Vergnügen, welches aus der Nachahmung, in so fern ich sie für die Sache selbst nehme, entsteht, und kann keinen Einfluß in dieses haben" (L-M, XVII, 99).

[8] Mendelssohn, *Schriften zur Philosophie, Aesthetik und Apologetik*, ed. Moritz Brasch (Leipzig, 1880), II, 107.

[9] *Moses Mendelssohn und die deutsche Aesthetik* (Königsberg, 1904), pp. 133-134. Although Goldstein's account of Mendelssohn's development conforms with my own assessment of the situation, I take strong exception to his interpretation of the position held by Lessing during the years 1756-57. On pp. 125-126 and 144, Goldstein maintains that Lessing endeavored to restrict the concept of illusion to the qualities communicated through theatrical performance in his correspondence with Mendelssohn and Nicolai at that time. However,

in these letters, Lessing is actually disputing the feasibility of establishing illusion in *any* of the imitative arts – including drama performed in the theater.
[10] See *Poetics*, 1455a, 24; 1462a, 18. The term "vividness" is Else's rendition of the Greek word "ἐναργέτατα."
[11] See the citation on p. 64 for an example of such usage.
[12] L-M, VIII, 216-217. Here in the article dated February 7, 1760, Lessing writes: "Das ist ohne Zweifel ein Hauptpunkt! Wir haben kein Theater. Wir haben keine Schauspieler. Wir haben keine Zuhörer. – Hören Sie, was ein neuer französischer Schriftsteller von diesem Punkte der Aufmunterung sagt: 'Eigentlich zu reden, sagt er, giebt es ganz und gar keine öffentlichen Schauspiele mehr. Was sind unsere Versammlungen in dem Schauplatze, auch an den allerzahlreichsten Tagen, gegen die Versammlungen des Volks zu Athen und zu Rom?... Wie viel Gewalt aber eine grosse Menge von Zuschauern habe, das kann man überhaupt aus dem Eindrucke, den die Menschen auf einander machen, und aus der Mittheilung der Leidenschaften abnehmen, die man bey Rebellionen wahrnimmt...'" Lessing's approbation of Diderot's remarks was drawn to my attention by the discussion on pp. 42-44 of Ursula Liebrecht Jarvis's unpubl. diss. previously cited in n. 1 of the present chapter. In view of this appeal to Diderot and other instances in which Lessing discounts the need for a total deception of the spectator's senses, Mrs. Jarvis concludes: "Had Lessing not used the traditional terminology of illusion at all, his statements would have gained immeasurably in clarity and consistency" (p. 54). Perhaps the same judgment is equally applicable to Mendelssohn's revised formulation of the concept as well.

NOTES VI: THE SUPERIORITY OF THE DRAMA

[1] L-M, XVII, 246. This citation constitutes additional evidence that Lessing believed the dramatic method to be independent of theatrical performance and that he consistently adhered to this principle ever since he first proposed it in his letter to Mendelssohn dated December 18, 1756.

[2] L-M, XVII, 247. In a footnote to this passage, the editors point out that over the word *sehe* in the original draft of this letter Lessing had written the word *erlebe*.

[3] Hamburger, *Die Logik der Dichtung*, 2nd ed. (Stuttgart, 1968), p. 61. The first edition of this work was published at Stuttgart in 1957.

[4] In an interview held on December 14, 1956, Thornton Wilder unequivocally declared his preference for the dramatic form by asserting: "A dramatist is one who believes that the pure event, an action involving human beings, is more arresting than any comment that can be made upon it. On the stage it is always now; the personages are standing on that razor-edge, between the past and the future, which is the essential character of conscious being; the words are rising to their lips in immediate spontaneity. A novel is what *took place*; no self-effacement on the part of the narrator can hide the fact that we hear his voice recounting, recalling events that are past and over, and which he has selected – from uncountable others – to lay before us from his presiding intelligence. Even the most objective novels are cradled in the authors' emotions and the authors' assumptions about life and mind and the passions ... The theater is supremely fitted to say: 'Behold! These things are.'" See *Writers at Work: The Paris Review Interviews*, ed. Malcolm Cowley (New York, 1958), pp. 108-109.

[5] Hamburger, pp. 172-173. In a generally sympathetic review of the first edition, Roy Pascal takes exception to Miss Hamburger's argument on the epic preterite by pointing out that the novelist's practice of using the historical present in order to render a narrative more

vivid would seem to indicate that "the present tense does have, in certain contexts, a more 'present' implication than the preterite." See "Tense and Novel," *Modern Language Review*, LVII (January 1962), 9.

[6] Hamburger, p. 154 (n. 109). The corresponding passage in the first edition is somewhat fuller and runs accordingly: "Er ist es, der erzählt, aber er erzählt nicht *von* seinen Gestalten (Dingen und Begebenheiten), sondern er erzählt die Gestalten, wie der Maler die seinigen malt. Und wie dieser zugleich indem er malt auch deutet, ohne daß der eine Vorgang von dem anderen zu trennen wäre, so erzählt der erzählende Dichter zugleich indem er deutet" (p. 113).

[7] *Poetics*, 1460a. Cf. Gustave Flaubert's observation in the letter to Mademoiselle Leroyer de Chantepie dated March 18, 1857: "L'artiste doit être dans son œuvre comme Dieu dans la création, invisible et tout-puissant; qu'on le sente partout, mais qu'on ne le voie pas."

[8] Since these remarks to Nicolai stress the importance of dramatic technique in Homer's epics, Lessing's interpretation of Aristotle's position fully conforms to the analysis set forth on pp. 620-621 of Else's commentary. However, some literary scholars have taken a different view of Aristotle's intent here. Kenneth A. Telford, for example, holds that Aristotle is merely condemning those passages in an epic poem in which the poet adds a personal commentary on the action and is not referring to the fact that the action is narrated by the poet. See Telford's translation and commentary entitled *Aristotle's Poetics* (Chicago, 1961), pp. 136-137.

[9] *Poetics*, 1449b. The omission indicated by the ellipsis marks in the above citation is Lessing's own.

[10] L-M, X, 111. Lessing holds the juxtaposition of "narration" and "pity and fear" to be of crucial importance and accuses other translators (such as Dacier and Curtius) of having distorted this aspect of

Aristotle's definition of tragedy. However, the antithesis between these concepts is considerably muted in most modern translations since the grammatical unit actually placed in opposition to "narration" is not "pity and fear," but rather a reference to the art of "acting." In Else's latest version of the *Poetics* (Ann Arbor, 1967), for example, this passage reads as follows: "Tragedy, then, is a process of imitating an action ... enacted by persons themselves and not presented through narrative; through a course of pity and fear completing the purification of tragic acts which have those emotional characteristics" (p. 25).

[11] L-M, X, 112. Among contemporary critics who distinguish between the dramatic, the epic, and the lyric modes of literary composition on the basis of temporal criteria, Emil Staiger is noteworthy for his decision not to equate present time with the dramatic method. Instead, he seems to associate the temporal quality of the dramatic mode with future, the epic mode with present, and the lyric mode with past time. In his *Grundbegriffe der Poetik* (Zürich, 1961), for example, Staiger observes: "Was der lyrische Dichter erinnert, vergegenwärtigt der epische ... Was der epische Dichter vergegenwärtigt, entwirft der dramatische" (pp. 218-219). Interestingly enough, on p. 113 of the *Grundbegriffe*, Staiger draws moral support for his claim concerning the future temporal reference of dramatic action by citing a line from one of the early drafts for *Laokoon*. Here Lessing writes: "Eine Reihe von Bewegungen, die auf einen Endzweck abzielen, heißet eine *Handlung*" (XIV, 37). However, to judge from the interpretation of Aristotle's definition of tragedy that is advanced in the *Dramaturgie*, Lessing himself appears to be formally committed to the idea of the drama's contemporaneity as contrasted with the epic's depiction of past events.

[12] "The Parable of the Rings in Lessing's *Nathan der*

Weise," *Germanic Review*, XXVI (December 1951), 259.

[13] In the forty-eighth article of the *Dramaturgie*, Lessing maintains that he is unconcerned whether any given play by Euripides is wholly a narrative or wholly a drama, but rather is interested solely in determining whether the poet has achieved the higher purpose which originally induced him to attempt a mixing of these genres. At the same time, however, Lessing acknowledges that Euripides often leaves himself open to censure for not having found a more subtle mode of conveying information to the audience than through the mouth of some Higher Being who has no direct connection with the action.

[14] *Der Briefwechsel zwischen Friedrich Schiller und Wilhelm von Humboldt*, ed. Siegfried Seidel (Berlin, 1962), II, 161-162. Humboldt himself appears to accept the validity of this distinction and utilizes it subsequently in his essay entitled *Über Goethes Hermann und Dorothea*. Here in 1799 Humbodt writes: "Nun ist der einfachste Unterschied zwischen Epopee und Tragödie unstreitig: die *vergangene* und die *gegenwärtige* Zeit" (*Werke*, ed. Andreas Flitner and Klaus Giel, II [Stuttgart, 1961], 272). It seems that René Wellek has overstated the uniqueness of the position taken by Humboldt in this passage when he recently declared: "Here apparently a coordination between the genres and time is asserted for the first time but the specific coordination was and is far from 'indisputable.' Humboldt makes no effort to relate the future to a genre and the lyric would, presumably, belong to the present ... The coordination with all three times is expressly carried out in Jean Paul's 'Vorschule der Ästhetik', in the second edition of 1813. The epic represents the event which develops from the past, the drama the action which extends toward the future, the lyric represents the emotion confined to the present." See pp. 405-406 of Wellek's article "Genre Theory, the

Lyric, and 'Erlebnis'," in *Festschrift für Richard Alewyn*, ed. Herbert Singer and Benno von Wiese (Köln, 1967).
[15] Recently, both works have been reissued in fascimile editions by the J. B. Metzlersche Verlagshandlung. See Johann Jakob Engel, *Über Handlung, Gespräch und Erzählung*, ed. Ernst Theodor Voss (Stuttgart, 1964) and Friedrich von Blanckenburg, *Versuch über den Roman*, ed. Eberhard Lämmert (Stuttgart, 1965).

NOTES VII: POETRY AS A MIMETIC ART

[1] In his article entitled "The Concept of Imitation in Modern Criticism," Haskell M. Block provides a general survey concerning the use and misuse of the mimetic principle among aesthetic theorists of the eighteenth century. See *Proceedings of the IVth Congress of the International Comparative Literature Association*, ed. François Jost (The Hague, 1966), II, 704-720.

[2] Hagstrum, *The Sister Arts: The Tradition of Literary Pictorialism and English Poetry from Dryden to Gray* (Chicago, 1958), pp. 9-10. For an excellent study of the theory of mimesis in ancient Greece, see Richard McKeon, "Literary Criticism and the Concept of Imitation in Antiquity," in *Critics and Criticism*, ed. R. S. Crane (Chicago, 1957), pp. 117-145.

[3] See the unpubl. diss. (Harvard, 1959), "Leibniz and Lessing's Critical Thought," p. 216.

[4] "Aesthetic Imitation and Imitators in Aristotle," *Philosophical Review*, XLV (November 1936), 564-565. Cf. Schopenauer's contention that music is a direct objectification of the will in *Die Welt als Wille und Vorstellung* (Bk. II, sec. 25).

[5] In the treatise *Lessing als ästhetischer Denker* (Göteborg, 1942), Folke Leander, for example, interprets modern aesthetics as a reaction against "imitation" in favor of "creativity" and maintains "in der [modernen] Ästhetik stellte man dem Abbilden das Neuschaffen, das Schöpferische gegenüber: der *Mimesis* die *Poiesis*" (p. 11). But in justice to Leander, it should be pointed out that he places Lessing in the modern category and states "daß sein Geist nicht in einem mimetischen, sondern in einem poietischen Verhältnis zur Wirklichkeit stand" (p. 41). He does not, however, make any attempt to reconcile this statement with the fact that Lessing himself held art to be an imitation of nature.

[6] "Aristotelian 'Mimesis' in Eighteenth Century England," *PMLA*, XXXVI (1921), 374.

[7] Burke, *A Philosophical Enquiry into the Origin of our*

Ideas of the Sublime and Beautiful, ed. J. T. Boulton (New York, 1958), pp. 172-173. In the prefatory materials to his translation of the *Poetics*, first published in 1789, Thomas Twining sets forth an interpretation of the concept of imitation which has much in common with the one proposed by Burke. Twining introduces his translation of the *Poetics* by two dissertations, one on poetical and the other on musical imitation. Within the first of these prefaces, which is entitled "On Poetry considered as an Imitative Art," Twining advances his own view that dramatic poetry is the only truly imitative mode of literature. Here he writes: "There seems to be but *one* view in which Poetry can be considered as *Imitation*, in the strict and proper sense of the word. If we look for both *immediate* and *obvious* resemblance, we shall find it only in *dramatic* – or to use a more general term – *personative* Poetry; that is, all Poetry in which, whether essentially or occasionally, the Poet personates; for here, *speech* is imitated by *speech* ... Now this is the case not only with the Tragic and Comic Poet, but also with the Epic Poet, and even the Historian, when either of these quits his own character, and *writes* a speech in the character of another person. He is then an imitator, in as strict a sense as the personal mimic. In *dramatic*, and all *personative* Poetry, then, both the conditions of what is *properly* denominated Imitation, are fulfilled." See *Aristotle's Treatise on Poetry*, 2nd ed. (London, 1812), I, 31-32.

[8] L-M, XVII, 138. Lessing first mentions the *Enquiry* in a letter to Nicolai dated November 25, 1757, where he states his intention of sending a copy of the book to Mendelssohn. In a subsequent letter to Mendelssohn dated January 21, 1758, he excuses himself for not having mailed the copy as yet on the grounds that he himself is in the process of translating it into German. At the outset of the letter to Mendelssohn dated February 18, 1758, he informs his friend that

the translation is for the most part already finished. Although Lessing refers to this translation again in the letter to Mendelssohn dated April 2, 1758, and in another to Karl Lessing dated October 28, 1768, the project was for some reason never carried through to completion. Unfortunately, scholars have only been able to locate a few pages of Lessing's translation. For details as to the fate of the remainder of the manuscript, see L-M, XIV, 220 (n. 1).

[9] "Burke among the Forerunners of Lessing," *PMLA*, XXII (1907, New Series XV), 625. Burke, it should be noted, does not appear to have regarded his own position on imitation to be independent of Aristotle. At the conclusion of a section in the *Enquiry* dealing with the topic of imitation, he himself remarks: "Aristotle has spoken so much and so solidly upon the force of imitation in his poetics, that it makes any further discourse upon this subject the less necessary." See *Enquiry*, p. 50 (Part I, sec. xvi). In the first dissertation preceding his translation of the *Poetics*, Twining, moreover, goes as far as to contend that Aristotle's treatise itself excludes descriptive poetry from the category of mimetic arts (p. 40). Whether Aristotle did in fact take this position in regard to descriptive poetry is debatable. But there can be little doubt that Twining is correct in his assertion "that [Aristotle] considered *dramatic* poetry as *peculiarly* imitative, above every other species" (p. 37).

[10] In the aforementioned article on Burke and Lessing, Howard himself completely overlooks the striking parallel between the views which the two men held in regard to dramatic poetry. Instead, his article concentrates on Burke's refutation of the aesthetic proposition *ut pictura poesis*. While conceding that Burke's conclusions are not formulated as systematically as those set forth in the sixteenth chapter of *Laokoon*, Howard goes on to remark: "But Burke had a clear notion of the difference between painting

and poetry, and of the appropriate means of expression in these arts ... The evidence before us would not seem to indicate that Lessing was especially influenced by Burke with respect to these matters. Nevertheless, he must have been confirmed by Burke in his instinctive abhorrence of descriptive poetry, and Burke's name deserves to be coupled with the names of Diderot and Mendelssohn as one of those who more or less definitely anticipated the conclusions reached in *Laokoon*" (p. 609).

BIBLIOGRAPHY

BIBLIOGRAPHY

I. PRIMARY SOURCES

Aristotle. *Poetics,* trans. Gerald F. Else. Ann Arbor, 1967.
Baumgarten, Alexander Gottlieb. *Reflections on Poetry,* ed. and trans. Karl Aschenbrenner and William H. Holther. Berkeley and Los Angeles, 1954.
Blanckenburg, Friedrich von. *Versuch über den Roman,* ed. Eberhard Lämmert. Stuttgart, 1965.
Burke, Edmund. *A Philosophical Enquiry into the Origin of our Ideas of the Sublime and Beautiful,* ed. J. T. Boulton. London and New York, 1958.
Dubos, Abbé. *Réflexions critique sur la poésie et sur la peinture,* quatrième édition revûë, corrigée & augmentée par l'Auteur. 3 vols. Paris, 1740.
Engel, Johann Jakob. *Über Handlung, Gespräch und Erzählung,* ed. Ernst Theodor Voss. Stuttgart, 1964.
Félibien, André. *Entretiens sur les vies et les ouvrages des plus excellens peintres anciens et modernes.* 6 vols. Trevoux, 1725.
Goethe, Johann Wolfgang von. *Gedenkausgabe der Werke, Briefe und Gespräche,* ed. Ernst Beutler. 24 vols. Zürich, 1948-1954.
- *Gespräche,* ed. F. and W. von Biedermann. 5 vols. Leipzig, 1909.
Gottsched, Johann Christoph. *Versuch einer Critischen Dichtkunst,* 4th ed. Leipzig, 1751.
Harris, James. *Three Treatises.* London, 1744.
Herder, Johann Gottfried. *Sämmtliche Werke,* ed. Bernhard Suphan. 33 vols. Berlin, 1877-1913.
Homer. *The Anger of Achilles: Homer's Iliad,* trans. Robert Graves. Garden City, N.Y., 1959.
Horace. *Satires, Epistles and Ars Poetica,* trans. H. Rushton Fairclough. Loeb Classical Library. New York and London, 1926.
Humboldt, Wilhelm von. *Werke,* ed. Andreas Flitner and Klaus Giel. 5 vols. Stuttgart, 1961-1970.

Kant, Immanuel. *Werke*, ed. Wilhelm Weischedel. 6 vols. Frankfurt, 1956-1964.
Leibniz, Gottfried Wilhelm. *Philosophical Papers and Letters*, trans. and ed. Leroy E. Loemker. 2 vols. Chicago, 1956.
Lessing, Gotthold Ephraim. *Sämtliche Schriften*, 3rd ed., ed. Karl Lachmann and Franz Muncker. 23 vols. Stuttgart and Leipzig, 1886-1924.
— *Werke*, ed. Julius Petersen and Waldemar von Olshausen. 25 vols. Berlin, 1925-1935.
Lessings Briefwechsel mit Mendelssohn und Nicolai über das Trauerspiel, nebst verwandten Schriften Nicolais und Mendelssohns, ed. Robert Petsch. Leipzig, 1910.
Mendelssohn, Moses. *Schriften zur Philosophie, Aesthetik und Apologetik*, ed. Moritz Brasch. 2 vols. Leipzig, 1880.
Schiller, Friedrich. *Der Briefwechsel zwischen Friedrich Schiller und Wilhelm von Humboldt*, ed. Siegfried Seidel. 2 vols. Berlin, 1962.
Twining, Thomas. *Aristotle's Treatise on Poetry, Translated: with Notes on the Translation and on the Original, and two Dissertations on Poetical and Musical Imitation*, 2nd ed. 2 vols. London, 1812.
Winckelmann, Johann Joachim. *Kleine Schriften-Vorreden-Entwürfe*, ed. Walter Rehm. Berlin, 1968.

II. SECONDARY WORKS ON LESSING

Allison, Henry E. *Lessing and the Enlightenment*. Ann Arbor, 1966.
Blümner, Hugo. Introduction and notes to *Lessings Laokoon*, 2nd ed. Berlin, 1880.
Cosack, Wilhelm. *Materialen zu Gotthold Ephraim Lessings Hamburgischer Dramaturgie*, 2nd ed. Paderborn, 1891.
Dobijanka, Olga. *Teoria Tragedii Lessinga*. Kraków, 1962.
Danzel, T. W. and G. E. Guhrauer. *Lessing: Sein Leben*

BIBLIOGRAPHY

und seine Werke, 2nd ed. 2 vols. Berlin, 1880-1881.
Drews, Wolfgang. *Lessing*. Rowohlts Monographien, no. 75. Reinbek bei Hamburg, 1962.
Droese, Detlef. *Lessing und die Sprache*. Zürich, 1968.
Folke, Leander. *Lessing als ästhetischer Denker*. Göteborg, 1942.
Frey, Adolf. *Die Kunstform des Lessingschen Laokoon.* Stuttgart und Berlin, 1905.
Garland, H. B. *Lessing: The Founder of Modern German Literature*, 2nd ed. London, 1962.
Gottschlich, Emil. *Lessing's aristotelische Studien*. Berlin, 1876.
Guthke, Karl S. *Der Stand der Lessing-Forschung: Ein Bericht über die Literatur von 1932-1962*. Stuttgart, 1965.
– and Heinrich Schneider. *Gotthold Ephraim Lessing.* Sammlung Metzler, no. 65. Stuttgart, 1967.
Hanson, Harlan Philip. "Leibniz and Lessing's Critical Thought." Unpubl. diss. Harvard, 1959.
Harald, Henry. *Herder und Lessing*. Würzburg, 1941.
Horovitz, Aurelie. *Beiträge zu Lessings Philosophie*. Bern, 1907.
Howard, William Guild. Introduction and notes to *Laokoon: Lessing, Herder, Goethe*. New York, 1910.
Kommerell, Max. *Lessing und Aristoteles*. Frankfurt, 1940.
Kont, J. *Lessing et l'antiquité*. 2 vols. Paris, 1894.
Krause, Siegfried. *Das Problem des Irrationalen in Lessings Poetik*. Diss. Köln, 1962.
Leisegang, Hans. *Lessings Weltanschauung*. Leipzig, 1931.
Leysaht, Konrad. *Dubos et Lessing*. Greifswald, 1874.
Mann, Otto. Introduction and notes to Lessing's *Hamburgische Dramaturgie*, 2nd ed. Kröners Taschenausgaben, no. 267. Stuttgart, 1963.
– *Lessing: Sein und Leistung*, 2nd ed. Hamburg, 1961.
May, Kurt. *Lessings und Herders kunsttheoretische Gedanken in ihrem Zusammenhang*. Berlin, 1923.

Metzger, Michael M. *Lessing and the Language of Comedy*. The Hague and Paris, 1966.
Nolte, Fred O. *Lessing's Laokoon*. Lancaster, Pa., 1940.
Oehlke, Waldemar. *Lessing und seine Zeit*. 2 vols. München, 1919.
Rehm, Walter. *Winckelmann und Lessing*. Berlin, 1941.
Rempel, Hans. *Tragödie und Komödie im dramatischen Schaffen Lessings*. Berlin, 1935.
Riemann, Robert. *Lessing*. Leipzig, 1910.
Rilla, Paul. *Lessing und sein Zeitalter*. Berlin, 1960.
Ritzel, Wolfgang. *Gotthold Ephraim Lessing*. Stuttgart, 1966.
Robertson, J. G. *Lessing's Dramatic Theory*. Cambridge, 1939.
Schmarsow, August. *Erläuterungen und Kommentar zu Lessings Laokoon*. Leipzig, 1907.
Schmidt, Erich. *Lessing*, 4th ed. 2 vols. Berlin, 1923.
Schneider, Heinrich. *Das Buch Lessing*, rev. ed. Bern, 1961.
– *Lessing: Zwölf biographische Studien*. Bern, 1951.
Schrempf, Christof. *Lessing als Philosoph*, 2nd ed. Stuttgart, 1921.
Schrimpf, Hans Joachim. *Lessing und Brecht: Von der Aufklärung auf dem Theater*. Pfullingen, 1965.
Seidel, Siegfried. *Gotthold Ephraim Lessing: Leben und Werk*. Berlin, 1963.
Steinmetz, Horst, ed. *Lessing – ein unpoetischer Dichter*. Frankfurt am Main and Bonn, 1969.
Szarota, Elida Maria. *Lessings "Laokoon."* Weimar, 1959.
Tschernyschewskij, N.G. *Fortschrittliche Ideen in der Ästhetik Lessings*. Düsseldorf, München, Hamburg, n.d.
Vail, Curtis C. D. *Lessing's Relation to the English Language and Literature*. New York, 1936.
Wiese, Benno von. *Lessing: Dichtung, Aesthetik, Philosophie*. Leipzig, 1931.
Witkowski, Georg. *Lessing*. Bielefeld-Leipzig, 1921.

III. OTHER SECONDARY WORKS

Althaus, Horst. *Laokoon: Stoff und Form.* Bern, 1968.
Atkins, J. W. H. *English Literary Criticism: 17th and 18th Centuries.* London, 1951.
Babbitt, Irving. *The New Laokoon.* Boston and New York, 1910.
Bate, Walter Jackson. *From Classic to Romantic.* Cambridge, Mass., 1946.
Baumann, Julius. *Wolffsche Begriffsbestimmungen.* Leipzig, 1910.
Bieber, Margarete. *Laocoon: The Influence of the Group since its Rediscovery,* rev. and enl. ed. Detroit, 1967.
Birke, Joachim. *Christian Wolffs Metaphysik und die zeitgenössische Literatur- und Musiktheorie: Gottsched, Scheibe, Mizler.* Berlin, 1966.
Blackall, Eric. *The Emergence of German as a Literary Language, 1700-1775.* Cambridge, 1959.
Blackmur, R. P. *Language as Gesture.* New York, 1952.
Bosanquet, Bernard. *A History of Aesthetic.* London and New York, 1932.
Bosshard, Walter. *Winckelmann: Aesthetik der Mitte.* Zürich and Stuttgart, 1960.
Boyd, John D. *The Function of Mimesis and Its Decline.* Cambridge, Mass., 1968.
Brooks, Van Wyck. *Fenollosa and His Circle.* New York, 1962.
Cassirer, Ernst. *An Essay on Man.* New Haven, 1944.
- *Die Philosophie der Aufklärung.* Tübingen, 1932.
- *Die Philosophie der symbolischen Formen.* 3 vols. Berlin, 1923-1929.
Clark, Robert. *Herder: His Life and Thought.* Berkeley and Los Angeles, 1955.
Cohen, Ralph. *The Art of Discrimination: Thomson's 'The Seasons' and the Language of Criticism.* London, 1964.
Cowley, Malcolm, ed. *Writers at Work: The Paris Review Interviews.* New York, 1958.

Croce, Benedetto. *Aesthetic*, trans. Douglas Ainslie, rev. ed. New York, 1922.
Daunicht, Richard. *Die Entstehung des bürgerlichen Trauerspiels in Deutschland*, 2nd ed. Berlin, 1965.
Davis, James Herbert. *Tragic Theory and the Eighteenth-Century French Critics*. University of North Carolina Studies in the Romance Languages and Literatures, no. 68. Chapel Hill, 1967.
Else, Gerald F. *Aristotle's Poetics: The Argument*. Cambridge, Mass., 1957.
Erdmann, Johannn Eduard. *Grundriß der Geschichte der Philosophie*, 4th ed. 2 vols. Berlin, 1896.
Fenollosa, Ernest. *The Chinese Written Character as a Medium for Poetry*, with foreword and notes by Ezra Pound. New York, n.d.
Folkierski, Wladyslaw. *Entre le classicisme et le romantisme*. Paris, 1925.
Friedemann, Käte. *Die Rolle des Erzählers in der Epik*. Berlin, 1910.
Fugate, Joe K. *The Psychological Basis of Herder's Aesthetics*. The Hague and Paris, 1966.
Gay, Peter. *The Enlightenment: An Interpretation*. 2 vols. New York, 1966-1969.
Gilbert, Katherine E. and Helmut Kuhn. *A History of Esthetics*. New York, 1939.
Goldstein, Ludwig. *Moses Mendelssohn und die deutsche Aesthetik*. Königsberg, 1904.
Gombrich, E. H. *Art and Illusion*. New York, 1960.
Gorelik, Mordecai. *New Theatres for Old*. New York, 1940.
Hagstrum, Jean H. *The Sister Arts: The Tradition of Literary Pictorialism and English Poetry from Dryden to Gray*. Chicago, 1958.
Hamburger, Käthe. *Die Logik der Dichtung*. Stuttgart, 1957.
– *Die Logik der Dichtung*, 2nd ed. Stuttgart, 1968.
Hatfield, Henry. *Aesthetic Paganism in German Literature. From Winckelmann to the Death of Goethe*. Cambridge, Mass., 1967.

BIBLIOGRAPHY

- *Winckelmann and His German Critics, 1755-1781.* New York, 1943.
Hazard, Paul. *European Thought in the Eighteenth Century From Montesquieu to Lessing.* Cleveland and New York, 1963.
Heitner, Robert R. *German Tragedy in the Age of Enlightenment.* Berkeley and Los Angeles, 1963.
Herrick, Marvin T. *The Poetics of Aristotle in England.* New Haven, 1930.
Hipple, Walter John. *The Beautiful, the Sublime, and the Picturesque in Eighteenth Century Aesthetic Theory.* Carbondale, Ill., 1957.
Ingarden, Roman. *Das literarische Kunstwerk*, 3rd ed. Tübingen, 1965.
- *Untersuchungen zur Ontologie der Kunst.* Tübingen, 1962.
Jarvis, Ursula Liebrecht. "Theories of Illusion and Distance in Drama: From Lessing to Brecht." Unpubl. diss. Columbia, 1961.
Jauß, Hans Robert, ed. *Nachahmung und Illusion.* Kolloquium Gießen, Juni 1963. München, 1964.
Justi, Carl. *Winckelmann und seine Zeitgenossen*, 4th ed. 2 vols. Leipzig, 1943.
Langer, Susanne K. *Feeling and Form.* New York, 1953.
- *Mind: An Essay on Human Feeling.* Vol. I. Baltimore, 1967.
- *Philosophy in a New Key*, 3rd ed. Cambridge, Mass., 1957.
- *Problems of Art.* New York, 1957.
Lee, Rensselaer W. *Ut Pictura Poesis: The Humanistic Theory of Painting.* New York, 1967.
Lempicki, Sigmund von. *Geschichte der deutschen Literaturwissenschaft bis zum Ende des 18. Jahrhunderts*, 2nd ed. Stuttgart, 1968.
Lockemann, Wolfgang. *Die Entstehung des Erzählproblems: Untersuchungen zur deutschen Dichtungstheorie im 17. und 18. Jahrhundert.* Meisenheim am Glan, 1963.

Lombard, A. *L'Abbé Du Bos, un initiateur de la pensée moderne.* Paris, 1913.
McLuhan, Marshall and Harley Parker. *Through the Vanishing Point: Space in Poetry and Painting.* New York, Evanston and London, 1968.
Markwardt, Bruno. *Geschichte der deutschen Poetik.* 5 vols. Berlin, 1956-1967.
Monk, Samuel H. *The Sublime: A Study of Critical Theories in XVIII-Century England.* New York, 1935.
Mortier, Roland. *Diderot en Allemagne 1750-1850.* Paris, 1954.
– *Diderot in Deutschland 1750-1850.* Verb. u. verm. Ausg. Trans. Hans G. Schürmann, Stuttgart, 1967.
Nicolson, Marjorie Hope. *Mountain Gloom and Mountain Glory: The Development of the Aesthetics of the Infinite.* Ithaca, N.Y., 1959.
Nivelle, Armand. *Les théories esthétiques en Allemagne de Baumgarten à Kant.* Paris, 1955.
Olson, Elder, ed. *Aristotle's Poetics and English Literature.* Chicago, 1965.
Pikulik, Lothar. *"Bürgerliches Trauerspiel" und Empfindsamkeit.* Köln, 1966.
Riemann, Albert. *Die Ästhetik Baumgartens.* Erlangen, 1928.
Rosenthal, Bronislawa. *Der Geniebegriff des Aufklärungszeitalters.* Berlin, 1933.
Ruttkowski, Wolfgang Victor. *Die literarischen Gattungen* Bern, 1968.
Schasler, Max. *Kritische Geschichte der Ästhetik.* 2 vols. Berlin, 1872.
Scherpe, Klaus. *Gattungspoetik im 18. Jahrhundert.* Stuttgart, 1968.
Spingarn, Joel E. *A History of Literary Criticism in the Renaissance,* 2nd ed. New York, 1908.
Staiger, Emil. *Grundbegriffe der Poetik.* Zürich, 1961.
Stein, Heinrich von. *Die Entstehung der neueren Ästhetik.* Stuttgart, 1886.

Stein, Jack M. *Richard Wagner and the Synthesis of the Arts.* Detroit, 1960.
Telford, Kenneth A. *Aristotle's Poetics.* Chicago, 1961.
Tuveson, Ernest Lee. *The Imagination as a Means of Grace: Locke and the Aesthetics of Romanticism.* Berkeley and Los Angeles, 1960.
Wellek, René. *A History of Modern Criticism: 1750-1950.* 4 vols. New Haven, 1955-1965.
– *The Rise of English Literary History.* Chapel Hill, 1941.
Whitmann, Cedric. *Homer and the Heroic Tradition.* Cambridge, Mass., 1958.
Wimsatt, William K. and Cleanth Brooks. *Literary Criticism: A Short History.* New York, 1959.

IV. ARTICLES IN BOOKS AND PERIODICALS

Atkins, Stuart. "The Parable of the Rings in Lessing's *Nathan der Weise*," *Germanic Review*, XXVI (December 1951), 259-267.
Block, Haskell M. "The Concept of Imitation in Modern Criticism," in *Proceedings of the IVth Congress of the International Comparative Literature Association*, ed. François Jost. The Hague, 1966, II, 704-720.
Davies, Cicely. "Ut Pictura Poesis," *Modern Language Review*, XXX (April 1935), 159-169.
Dickson, K. A. "Lessing's Creative Misinterpretation of Aristotle," *Greece and Rome*, XIV (April 1967), 53-60.
Dieckmann, Herbert. "Esthetic Theory and Criticism in the Enlightenment," in *Introduction to Modernity*, ed. Robert Mollenauer. Austin, 1965, pp. 63-105.
Dilthey, Wilhelm. "Gotthold Ephraim Lessing," in Wilhelm Dilthey, *Das Erlebnis und die Dichtung*, 13th ed. Stuttgart and Göttingen, 1957, pp. 11-110.
Draper, John W. "Aristotelian 'Mimesis' in Eighteenth Century England," *PMLA*, XXXVI (1921), 372-400.
– "Poetry and Music in Eighteenth Century Aes-

thetics," *Englische Studien*, LVII (1932-33), 70-85.
Erhardt-Siebold, Erika von. "The Harmony of the Senses," *PMLA*, XLVIII (June 1932), 577-592.
Friedrich, Wolf-Hartmut. "Sophokles, Aristoteles und Lessing," *Euphorion*, LVII (1963), 4-27.
Gilbert, Katherine E. "Aesthetic Imitation and Imitators in Aristotle," *Philosophical Review*, XLV (November 1936), 558-573.
Gillet, Joseph E. "The Catharsis-Clause in German Criticism before Lessing," *The Journal of Philology*, XXXV (1920), 95-112.
– "Wesen und Wirkungsmittel des Dramas in Deutschland vor Gottsched," *Modern Philology*, XVII (February 1920), 141-156.
Goddard, Eunice R. "Psychological Reasons for Lessing's Attitude toward Descriptive Poetry," *PMLA*, XXVI (1911, New Series XIX), 593-603.
Gombrich, E. H. "Lessing," *Proceedings of the British Academy*, XLIII (1957), 133-156.
Heitner, Robert. "A Gottschedian Reply to Lessing's Seventeenth *Literaturbrief*," in *Studies in Germanic Languages and Literatures: In Memory of Fred O. Nolte*, ed. Erich Hofacker and Liselotte Dieckmann. St. Louis, 1963, pp. 43-58.
Heller, Peter. "Lessing: The Virtuoso of the Dialectic," in Peter Heller, *Dialectics and Nihilism*. Amherst, Mass., 1966, pp. 1-68.
Howard, William Guild. "Burke among the Forerunners of Lessing," *PMLA*, XXII (1907, New Series XV), 608-632.
– "Goethe's Essay *Über Laokoon*," *PMLA*, XXI (1906, New Series XVII), 930-944.
– "Reiz ist Schönheit in Bewegung," *PMLA*, XXIV (1909, New Series XVII), 286-293.
– "Ut Pictura Poesis," *PMLA*, XXIV (1909, New Series XVII), 40-123.
Linn, Marie-Luise. "A. G. Baumgartens 'Aesthetica' und die antike Rhetorik," *Deutsche Vierteljahrsschrift*

für Literaturwissenschaft und Geistesgeschichte, XLI (1967), 424-443.

McKeon, Richard. "Literary Criticism and the Concept of Imitation in Antiquity," in *Critics and Criticism*, ed. R. S. Crane. Chicago, 1957, pp. 117-145.

Mayer, Hans. "Lessing, Mitwelt und Nachwelt," in Hans Mayer, *Von Lessing bis Thomas Mann*. Pfullingen, 1959, pp. 79-109.

— "Lessing und Aristoteles," in *Festschrift für Bernhard Blume*, ed. Egon Schwarz, Hunter G. Hannum, and Edgar Lohner. Göttingen, 1967, pp. 61-75.

Michelsen, Peter. "Die Erregung des Mitleids durch die Tragödie: Zu Lessings Ansichten über das Trauerspiel im Briefwechsel mit Mendelssohn und Nicolai," *Deutsche Vierteljahrsschrift für Literaturwissenschaft und Geistesgeschichte*, XL (1966), 548-566.

Morgan, Charles. "The Nature of Dramatic Illusion," in *Reflections on Art*, ed. Susanne K. Langer. Baltimore, 1958, pp. 91-102.

Munteano, B. "Survivances antique: L'abbé Du Bos esthéticien," *Revue de littérature comparée*, XXX (1956), 318-350.

Nolte, Fred O. "Lessing's Correspondence with Mendelssohn and Nicolai," *Harvard Studies and Notes in Philology and Literature*, XIII (1931), 309-332.

Pascal, Roy. "Tense and Novel," *Modern Language Review*, LVII (January 1962), 1-11.

Ritzel, Wolfgang. "Lessings Denkformen," *Kant Studien*, LVII (1964-1966), 155-166.

Schadewaldt, Wolfgang. "Furcht und Mitleid – Zu Lessings Deutung des Aristotelischen Tragödiensatzes," *Deutsche Vierteljahrsschrift für Literaturwissenschaft und Geistesgeschichte*, XXX (1956), 137-140.

Sichtermann, Hellmut. "Lessing und die Antike," in *Lessing und die Zeit der Aufklärung*. Veröffentlichung der Joachim Jungius-Gesellschaft der Wissenschaften (Hamburg). Göttingen, 1968, pp. 168-193.

Staiger, Emil. "Dialektik der Begriffe Originalität und Nachahmung," in *Tradition und Ursprünglichkeit*, ed. Werner Kohlschmidt and Herman Meyer. Bern, 1966, pp. 29-38.

Stamm, Israel. "Herder and the *Aufklärung:* A Leibnizian Context," *Germanic Review*, XXXVIII (May 1963), 197-208.

Teuber, Eugen. "Die Kunstphilosophie des Abbé Dubos," *Zeitschrift für Ästhetik und allgemeine Kunstwissenschaft*, XVII (1924), 361-410.

Vail, Curtis C. D. "Lessing's Attitude toward Storm and Stress," *PMLA*, LXV (September 1950), 805-823.

Wecter, Dixon. "Burke's Theory of Words, Images, and Emotion," *PMLA*, LV (March 1940), 167-181.

Wellek, René. "Genre Theory, the Lyric, and 'Erlebnis,'" in *Festschrift für Richard Alewyn*, ed. Herbert Singer and Benno von Wiese. Köln, 1967, pp. 392-412.

Wichelns, Herbert A. "Burke's Essay on the Sublime and its Reviewers," *Journal of English and Germanic Philology*, XXI (1922), 645-661.

Wittkower, Rudolf. "Imitation, Eclectism, and Genius," in *Aspects of the Eighteenth Century*, ed. Earl R. Wasserman. Baltimore, 1965, pp. 143-161.

Ziolkowski, Theodore. "Language and Mimetic Action in Lessing's *Miss Sara Sampson*," *Germanic Review*, XL (November 1965), 261-276.

www.ingramcontent.com/pod-product-compliance
Lightning Source LLC
Chambersburg PA
CBHW031315150426
43191CB00005B/241